To chase a dream

TO CHASE **A DREAM**

A SOCCER CHAMPIONSHIP, AN UNLIKELY HERO
AND A JOURNEY THAT REDEFINED WINNING

Alex –

Chase your dreams!

Whitey

British Library Cataloguing in Publication Data
A catalogue record for this book is available from the British Library

To chase a dream
Maidenhead: Meyer & Meyer Sport (UK) Ltd., 2014
ISBN: 978-1-78255-019-8

© 2014 by Meyer & Meyer Sport (UK) Ltd.
Auckland, Beirut, Budapest, Cairo, Cape Town, Dubai, Hägendorf, Indianapolis,
Maidenhead, Singapore, Sydney, Tehran, Wien
Member of the World Sport Publishers' Association (WSPA)
Printed by: Color House Graphics
ISBN: 978-1-78255-019-8
E-Mail: info@m-m-sports.com
www.m-m-sports.com

CONTENTS

FOREWORD

I met Paul Kapsalis in the fall of his senior year in high school, when I presented him with the award for best defensive player of the Indiana high school state soccer tournament. Nice kid, I thought. And that was about it.

When he called a few months later to ask about his chances of playing at Indiana University, I wanted to be kind. And, the kindest thing I could do was be honest. I told him he had no chance. When he shocked me a few weeks later and said he was going to try out at Indiana, ditching his plans to play somewhere else, I was honest again. "No promises," I said, "but you can take your chances with the rest of the guys who show up for tryouts." Those prospects were very bleak, to say the least.

Even after he made the team by the skin of his teeth, I placed him at the very bottom of our 35-player roster, figuring he'd quit. He was undersized, not very athletic and simply lacked that special talent we looked for at IU.

I couldn't have been more wrong about that assessment, and couldn't be more grateful.

Almost any coach can see physical talent pretty quickly. Heart and character aren't always evident. Those can take time to emerge. Looking back on Whitey's journey, I think his heart and character were fairly obvious from the outset. It just took me a while to see.

What I discovered was that this nice, bright-eyed kid has the heart of a lion and the leadership skills any coach covets in a player.

Even when, finally, I found that I desperately needed him to set an example—by his leadership, positive attitude, work ethic and persistence—I wasn't so sure I needed him to play. But Paul convinced me of that, too.

Maybe Paul's rough road—sitting out year after year and being repeatedly told he wasn't good enough; being encouraged to transfer; suffering a year-long, career-threatening injury—was what gave him that character and heart. Maybe his odyssey was something of a test.

The result? You can read all the details in the pages that follow. I'll just say that he turned out to be one of the best leaders I've coached. I frankly wouldn't have believed it if I hadn't lived it. Twenty five years later, I still shake my head and marvel at what this happy, determined kid was able to accomplish, what he meant to Indiana Soccer, and what an inspirational example he sets for everyone, of all ages, in athletics and in life. I'm guessing you'll feel the same way.

Jerry Yeagley

Coach, Indiana University Men's Soccer, 1973-2003, winner of six national championships; five-time NCAA Coach of the Year; National Soccer Hall of Fame inductee

1

Me, Deanne, Pete, Dean and Dan get ready for our first season in Edina, MN.

THE NEW FAMILY PASTIME

CHAPTER 1:

THE NEW FAMILY PASTIME

Baseball was supposed to be my passion.

It certainly was our family passion. We're Chicago Cubs fans. But, the Cubs being what they are, perennial "lovable losers," maybe it was divine mercy that directed me somewhere else. Maybe it was dumb luck, or maybe it was for another reason I wouldn't understand until almost two decades later.

But, at age 5, soccer became my game. Our family moved for the second time in what would be five times to accommodate my dad's career, a move that dropped all of us in suburban St. Louis, where my dad looked to register his kids in a baseball league.

In our family of four boys and a girl, sports always were a big part of our lives, and I was the middle child, which meant I was right in the middle of everything. We had a lot of energy and sports weren't only a way to burn off all that energy. They also were the vehicle our parents used to get us kids acclimated to a new town and to make friends in those new towns. It became our routine. We'd move in and my dad would sign us up for baseball, often before we'd finished unpacking. It was pretty effective, and I guess it was lucky for my parents that all of us kids loved sports.

But this time, in moving to Collinsville, Illinois, nine miles from St. Louis, my dad was about to be thrown a curve ball. He drove to a park where youth sports volunteers had set up card tables. It was the fall, and he asked what sports they offered. They said soccer. He said what else?

My dad's only recollection of soccer was from his high school days, back in the 1950s at Amundsen High School on Chicago's North Side. "Foreigners" used to play it around the school fields, and my dad and his friends poked fun at them because they wore short pants and communicated in foreign languages. Andy Kapsalis was a great athlete who loved basketball, baseball, and football. Way back then, in his youth, and as he stood there at the soccer league registration table in Collinsville, he thought, *what kind of sport doesn't involve catching the ball?*

He would, of course, change his mind completely in a few weeks, going on to help establish youth soccer leagues, helping my mom create a highly successful soccer retail business, and becoming one very enthusiastic soccer fan. But, at that moment, in Collinsville, kids' baseball leagues were six months away, and he wanted his kids to play an organized team game immediately.

He figured soccer was a team sport in which we could burn off all that energy and make friends. He registered his kids right there. Like many of my dad's instincts, he was right.

Almost immediately, my mom went out and bought a soccer ball. We inflated it, tossed it in the back yard and started kicking. We didn't know the rules. My parents didn't know the rules, but we knew how to kick a ball and after a few days, we set up a crude soccer pitch in our back yard, using t-shirts and cones—whatever we could find—to mark goals. Being brothers, we pounded the snot out of each other and, playing every day, slowly became decent players. My dad even joined us on weekends and one Sunday, broke his ankle. Even that wouldn't dampen his love for the game.

We also started playing hockey, but soccer was my first sport. I remember wanting to play all the time, totally absorbing everything coaches were dishing out. Love at first kick. The running, being outdoors on beautiful green grass, the high-level of teamwork, the grace, the power, the struggle, the competition—all of it resonated deep inside me and brought me such joy and release. I suppose it's the same way with a lot of folks when they find their calling: musicians and painters, writers and scientists, teachers and mathematicians. They must feel it in their marrow almost instantly.

I made the local tykes all-star team and got to play in Busch Stadium before the St. Louis Stars, the city's professional soccer team, played a game. There I was, a squirt of five years old, walking in that stadium. The thrill was indescribable. Then we walked through the dugout on the field and a very familiar emotion flared in me: nervousness, anxiety bordering on fear; knowing deep inside that I had to give it everything I had to compete. That feeling was something that stayed with me throughout my playing career, and, looking back, it may have helped as much as it hurt.

The giant stadium engulfed me; overwhelmed all of us, really. We must have looked like ants; sure felt like it. But that didn't matter to me or, I'd guess, to any of the other kids. When the game ended 1-1, we were greeted and congratulated by St. Louis Stars players. That was it for me. I was hooked totally and was going to chase soccer for as long as I could.

Two years later, my short career looked finished. My dad got transferred and moved us again, this time to Edina, Minnesota, a community with a lot going for it, but no youth soccer league. We could have gone back to baseball, but my parents saw the spark that soccer had ignited in their kids. So, mom and dad made a league of their own. The Edina Soccer Association was launched with 16 teams, allowing all five of us Kapsalis kids to play. Establishing that league made my parents look like prophets. They got out in front of what would be the wave of youth soccer popularity sweeping across the U.S. That's also where I got my nickname, Whitey. My dad gave it to me. Of all my parents' children, I was the only one who didn't have dark brown hair. Guess what color mine was? That's right, an almost white blond. We're still trying to figure out that one.

Four years later, we moved again, this time to Birmingham, Michigan, near Detroit, which did have a youth soccer league, and my parents wanted to register us. But, we arrived in the winter so my dad arranged for us to join the local hockey league.

The problem was that the hockey season had started a few weeks before we showed up. I can remember when my dad was helping me get dressed in the locker room for my first game. I was playing in an age group a year older and could hear some of the guys muttering to themselves about this new kid. I was much smaller than everybody else, my helmet barely visible above the boards, and in this new environment, felt a little like an invader, an unwanted visitor who the other guys thought was going to upset team chemistry. I hated it and as I trudged toward the rink, I told my dad I didn't want to go out there, didn't want to sit on the bench, and certainly didn't want to get on the ice with these guys. I was really intimidated.

"You'll be fine once you get on the ice," he told me. "You've got nothing to lose. Just try it today. If after the game, you don't like it, we're done. Over. Finished. You don't have to come back. No big deal. But you've got your skates on, all the gear, just get out there and try it."

He made a pretty persuasive argument. So, I clonked ahead on my own and those first few minutes on the bench, I ignored all the muttering from my teammates, but I was scared. No other way to say it. My dad joined my mom in the stands and they later told me that when I took the ice, all the parents were saying things like, "What's that little guy doing out there? He's going to get hurt. This is ridiculous. What's the coach thinking?" He and my mom sat there, steaming but silent.

I don't really remember my mindset when I pushed onto the ice. I'm sure I had that fear and anxiety, but I also was one competitive little guy, and I knew how to play hockey. Heck, I'd been playing in Minnesota, where it's religion, for about four years.

Well, I scored a goal in the first couple of minutes. Funny how that changed everybody's perspective. From that point on, when I took the ice, the parents started saying, "Here he comes, our secret weapon." Suddenly, my teammates rallied around me like I was their little brother. My mom says that was one of the first times I demonstrated the ability to draw people together, my first moment of leadership. I'm not sure of all that, but I had a whole lot of fun playing hockey with those guys, and I think they felt the same about me. That's all that really mattered to me then.

The other thing that one moment did was teach me to confront my fears. I'm so grateful my dad gave me that extra nudge to take the ice. I overcame all the uncertainty and, when I proved I was capable, my confidence grew. I knew I could handle more than I had thought I could, something I think all of us need to realize about ourselves. Those first few moments on that hockey team, as imperceptible as it was to everybody else, were enormously significant in my life.

And, the quiet confidence that experience created in me transferred to soccer in Birmingham, where our passion for the game deepened and became nearly all-consuming. Weather permitting, we played every day after school in our back yard or at a local park, like we had at our earlier homes.

A couple years after we moved there, Detroit entered the professional North American Soccer League, establishing the Detroit Express in about 1978, and my family became huge fans. All of us attended every home game in the old Pontiac Silverdome. Those were some of the most fun family times I can recall.

Watching professional soccer live on a regular basis also stoked our dreams. In the back yard we'd imitate our favorite players: Keith Furphy, Trevor Francis, Alan Brazil, Dave Shelton, and a handful of others. We were big fans of Shelton. One of only three Americans on the Express roster, he played at Indiana University, a place we'd never heard of until then. We knew nothing about college soccer but figured Indiana University must be a pretty decent team if Dave Shelton played there.

Those family outings were an example of a broader practice my family embraced, one that would serve me well throughout my life, in and out of soccer; serve my siblings, too. Growing up, we all went to each other's activities, no matter what the event. It could be Danny's baseball game on a Tuesday, Deanne's dance recital on a Saturday, Dean's soccer game on a Friday. All seven of us would pile in the car and head to the event. We showed our support by showing up for our brothers and sister. Maybe it grew from all those times we uprooted ourselves and moved to a new town. Throughout all that upheaval, the one constant we could hold on to was each other. Now, I realize how rare that was—and is—and how much of a blessing that was, and I'm so grateful my parents set that practice in motion. It formed a really strong, cool support network that we still use to this day.

As time passed, it became clear that the youth soccer league in Birmingham had a wide range of talent. My parents decided to try a new idea: a travelling program that would serve as something of a training academy/development league for the Express. One of the Express owners, John Maxwell, also owned the Bonanza Steakhouse chain, and he wanted to create a feeder program for the pro team. So, my parents—mostly my mom—created the Bonanza Express Soccer League. Under that setup, kids from each of six counties would try out for their county's team, which would travel throughout the region playing the other county teams. The Detroit Express assigned a player to each youth team, and that player would hold clinics. It was a way to give kids who were a little more serious about the sport an outlet to play in a more competitive format. It also was a badge of distinction to say you played for the Express development team. For my brothers and me—and probably the few dozen other kids on Bonanza Express teams—it fueled dreams of playing professionally.

That was one development in a Birmingham soccer experience that seemed to get better and better. I was a freshman at Groves High School when my oldest brother Pete made a dream come true: playing soccer at Michigan State University. Pete breaking through to that level made all of us dream that we could play soccer in college, too. I made up my mind then and there that I was going to finish at Groves and follow Pete at State.

Then everything crashed.

My dad came home one day and announced he had been promoted and transferred to Indianapolis. To say I was devastated would be an understatement. I was entering my sophomore year, during which I was pretty confident I'd play at the varsity level at Groves, my next step toward playing at Michigan State. I had a wide network of friends, a nice girlfriend.

Now, my parents were asking me to start all over again. It was too overwhelming. I all but refused to go. "India-no-place" was the last place I wanted to live.

As angry as I was, I thought my older brother Danny would be even more upset. He was varsity co-captain as a junior on a team that was highly ranked in Michigan and expected to be very competitive the following season. Groves' coach Guido Reggelburgge liked Danny so much that he offered to house him for his senior year if Danny would stay. He was going to take the coach up on the offer, but eventually decided to come with us.

That decision had almost everything to do with Indiana University. Danny knew that Indianapolis was about 55 miles north of Bloomington, Indiana, home of the Indiana University Hoosiers, where that boyhood hero of ours, Detroit Express' Dave Shelton, played college soccer. Since meeting Dave and reading about IU soccer, my brother had dreamed of playing there. This move, Danny thought, brought him one step closer.

We were scheduled to hit the road in June, and I was having a really hard time; really depressed about the whole thing, refusing to concede that I was leaving my life in Michigan. I held out hope of staying there and doing an extended version of the idea proposed to Danny: living with a family friend for three years of high school. It was nuts, of course. My parents, who've always been thoughtful, struggled with how to handle my despair, but they weren't about to leave me.

When we arrived in Carmel, Indiana, a suburb of Indianapolis, they decided to follow our previous strategy and contacted the local high school soccer coach, Bob Boots, which always struck me as a great last name for a soccer coach.

He agreed to meet us on a Sunday afternoon at his church. The four of us—Coach Boots, my dad, Danny, and I—met on folding chairs in the church community room. Coach Boots, a very unassuming, soft-spoken, deeply religious man, was cordial and smiled a lot, but I could tell he wasn't anywhere near as enthusiastic to meet us as we were to meet him. He was almost apathetic about it.

"We've got a lot of kids in the program here and a really competitive, strong team," he said. "Do you know what you boys are getting into?"

In fairness to him, he didn't know what he was looking at. He understood our predicament but he wanted to be very clear that this team was no shaggy collection of kids from the neighborhood. It was serious. Guys practiced hard and played to win. In fact, they were having an informal scrimmage later that afternoon, Coach Boots told us, and this was almost two months before the season.

"You're welcome to head over there and check it out," Coach Boots said. "See what you're up against."

That was one of those moments that stays with me to this day, a small but very powerful moment, and one that proved to be valuable throughout my playing career and life. Danny and I looked at each other. We were in street clothes—t-shirts, worn tennis shoes; me in white painters pants; Danny in blue jeans. And we thought, *No way are we stepping on the field for the first time looking like this and mixing it up with a bunch of top notch players. We'd look like idiots and then get our heads handed to us.*

And, yet, like I said before, I'm pretty competitive in my own quiet way. So are my brothers. We always have been. Like me, they were modest about it, but we all knew how to play the game and play hard, and we loved soccer. Loved it down to the calluses on our feet. We weren't about to back down.

Still, we saw this entry as all wrong. The guys on the Carmel team wouldn't know what the heck was going on—Coach Boots didn't attend the off-season workouts—and they'd view us as intruders, not teammates. They'd make fun of us for sure.

This was where my dad's foresight again was dead-on. He told us this might be the only real shot we get; that this setting, before the official practices start in August, would be an informal way to introduce us to the guys, give us a head start on making friends, and show everyone that we belonged. He had all the confidence in the world that we could play at their level. My dad always has believed in his kids, or at least he always led us to believe he believed in us.

So, we rolled up to this elementary school parking lot in our van. On the field behind the building, about 20 guys scrimmaged. After a few minutes of Danny and me wringing our hands and my dad prodding us to get out there, the two of us in our street clothes stepped out. The guys looked at us exactly the way I thought they would—like we were intruders. It was pretty humiliating and awkward, but we explained why we were there and they let us join the scrimmage.

Coach Boots was right. Carmel players were tough. But guess what? So were we.

From the moment I kicked the ball, the anxiety dissolved. The soccer field always represented a place where my brothers and I could escape the pressures of school, relationships, whatever, and immerse ourselves in the exhilaration of this beautiful game. It was where I felt the most like myself; the most comfortable.

Danny made a tremendous impact, scoring something like six goals in 45 minutes, and I hung in there, too. After, soaked in sweat and laughing about our soccer fashion statement, we climbed back in the van.

"That wasn't too bad, was it guys?" my dad said.

We were pretty confident we'd do just fine on Carmel's soccer team; maybe even lead the team on a deep run in the state tournament. And the guys on the team were pretty fired up to have us.

We went to the rest of the regular practices, and I made varsity as a sophomore. Danny had a monster year, setting the Carmel High School record for goals scored in a single season and leading the Greyhounds all the way to the regional finals. A great senior season.

I still felt a little out of place at Carmel, and Danny didn't get the attention from college coaches he'd hoped for, largely because high school soccer in Indiana didn't measure up to the caliber of play in other states like Illinois and Missouri. But, he was determined to play at Indiana University. So, he worked out hard, enrolled, and tried out for the team. When he was cut, we were all pretty bummed. I thought if Danny can't make it, IU must be top of the mountain.

As time passed, I settled in at Carmel. My junior year, we had a really strong team that made it all the way to the semi-finals of the state championship, and I was named Best Defensive Player in the tournament, an award handed to me by a guy named Jerry Yeagley, who, unbeknownst to me at the time, would become one of the key figures in my life. Jerry Yeagley was coach of the Indiana Hoosiers.

Imposing is the word that comes immediately to my mind when I think of him. Coach Yeagley was very polished, warm, articulate, good looking, and clean cut, dressed crisply in Adidas soccer gear in the cream and crimson of IU.

After the final game, I stood there on the field with my team and the other three teams in the tournament, and the public address announcer called players who were given honors. You'd step forward when your name was called, and coach would shake your hand.

I remember feeling this very definite presence, something very powerful when I stepped forward to shake his hand. Jerry Yeagley was the man.

"Congratulations," he told me. "You had a spectacular tournament."

The coach of Indiana University acknowledged me, and it felt like he meant it. It was a wow moment, but very brief, maybe five seconds. The public address announcer moved on to the next name and so did Coach Yeagley.

My senior season was another strong one. The Greyhounds got all the way to the state final, losing to North Central High School, and I was one of the team leaders.

Michigan State had expressed interest in me, offering a partial scholarship, and I committed quicker than you can say, "Go Sparty." Although I'd lost touch a bit with my friends in Michigan, I was looking forward to getting reacquainted and taking on the challenge of trying to play at Michigan State.

Meanwhile, Danny had trained extremely hard and given it one more shot at Indiana University. This time, he made the team. Our family went bonkers. Danny had worked and worked and worked and was in the best shape of his life, mentally and physically. To watch him accomplish that goal after all that effort thrilled us beyond belief. We were so proud of him. As it turns out, again unperceived by me, he was providing an incredible example.

The year went on and Danny climbed his way up the team roster and saw some playing time. Making the one and a half hour drive down to Bloomington to watch his games was really fun for our family, as were my occasional weekend solo visits. We'd talk about the soccer team, some of the players, what it was like to travel, to wear the IU jersey, to play for Coach Yeagley, a bunch of stuff. Most thrilling of all maybe was that IU went on to with the national championship that year, beating Duke University in the 8th overtime.

It was then that I started to appreciate what IU soccer was all about. Pick your sport and you can make the comparison. IU is to college soccer what Kansas or Duke is to college basketball; what the Pittsburgh Steelers or New England Patriots are to pro football; what the New York Yankees… nah, we're a lot more likable than them. But you get the idea.

IU has won eight national titles in men's soccer, made it to the title game a mind-blowing 14 times, been in the soccer version of the NCAA Final Four, known as the College Cup, 18 times, and has the NCAA's best record in the College Cup: 20 wins; 10 losses. Overall, the Hoosiers have amassed a winning percentage of .800. That, my friends, is what's known as a powerhouse.

Sometime in my brother's championship season, a little spark of a question flared in the deepest recesses of my mind. *What would it be like to play at IU?* I laughed. Who was I kidding? I'd already committed to Michigan State and was fired up about getting there and giving it my best shot. Besides, I was nowhere near the stature of the typical soccer Adonis who takes the field for IU.

Then, one day over the winter, I was shopping at a local mall and noticed that a TV in a lounge area was showing a replay of the national championship game against Duke. I look back on that now and think about how weird it was. No promotion. No IU gear for sale. Nothing. Just a TV set up, replaying the game and no one else there. It was kind of eerie. I'd never seen anything like that before or since. I hate shopping so I didn't need much of an incentive to watch for a few seconds. Then I sat on the couch and watched for a few minutes. Then I watched the entire thing.

It was crazy, sitting there for a couple of hours, totally absorbed. I wasn't cheering or whooping or shouting at the refs for making a bad call or calling out players' names. I was simply mesmerized, locked in, whatever you want to call it. And, here's the weirdest part: while taking in the game on this screen in front of me, all alone, I actually could see myself on the field, playing for IU, almost as if by some computer generated graphic editing I'd been inserted in the lineup. Looking back now, it kind of creeps me out, but the vision is very clear to this day.

The game ended—Yeah! IU won again!—and I thought, *What the heck? What would it hurt to send an application to Indiana?* I'd already applied and been accepted at MSU. This was just another form to fill out. So, I did apply. Several weeks later, I received a letter that I was accepted, which fueled my uncertainty.

Over the spring, I played club soccer and had a strong season. That set me up mentally and physically to train hard for college ball at Michigan State. But that performance also made me wonder more about whether I could play at IU. That goofy, surreal vision of me on the field during that national championship refused to rest. I started feeling this almost hypnotic pull. I loved IU's cream and crimson uniforms and the team-focused, hard-nosed style the Hoosiers brought to the field of battle. I loved the excellence, and I was intrigued by Coach Yeagley's persona. I loved the campus. I wanted to try to reach the pinnacle.

I decided to do something about it and wrote to Coach Yeagley to set up a meeting to chat about my chances. His responses were very clear. I didn't have a realistic chance of even making the team, let alone playing for the Hoosiers. But he agreed to meet.

So, one summer weekday, my mom and I jumped in the van and drove down. The entire route along Highway 37 was nerve wracking. Except for that one brief moment where he gave me a plaque, and maybe a couple times he saw me hanging out with Danny at IU, I didn't know Jerry Yeagley and he didn't know me, and he was one very intimidating guy. Not that he was a bully, he just carried himself with such confidence and was so polished.

On the drive, I kept thinking I should turn around and head back. I had no idea what I would say or what we would talk about. I wanted to play at IU and I didn't. I wanted him to beg me to join the team but I was thoroughly excited about — not to mention committed to — going back to Michigan and playing at State; a returning hero. Thoughts were swirling around my mind. Things seemed so jumbled.

We pulled up at the horseshoe driveway outside Assembly Hall and Coach Yeagley met me in the lobby. He was exactly the way I remembered him from the state tournament. Somebody once referred to him as the Godfather of college soccer and that surely fits.

He shook my hand, said my name, thanked me for coming down, and then got right to it.

"What can I do for you?"

That was the question I feared the most. I wanted him to say, "You know, Whitey, my boy, I've thought about it. Come on down and we'll get you a spot on the team and everything's going to be great. Can't wait to have you as a Hoosier."

But, he'd blown right past that fantasy, crashing it like a plate glass window.

"Well," I said, clearing my throat to loosen up the choking sensation taking hold, "coach, I just wanted to reiterate my interest in playing."

He reiterated his position and was very definitive about one thing: I had no business playing for Indiana University. I shouldn't even waste my time thinking about it. Coach Yeagley was very polite but direct, and I appreciated that.

"I'm sure you're aware we just won a national championship, Whitey," he told me, "and we've got seven starters coming back from that team. On top of that, son, we've got one of the best recruiting classes I've ever had coming here in a few weeks. To be honest with you, and just between you and me, I think we've got a real decent shot at winning the whole thing again."

He paused to get my attention and looked me in the eyes.
"Whitey, you're a real nice kid and a decent high school soccer player, and I don't want to mislead you. You're just not talented enough to play here."

I knew what he meant, and I started to feel foolish for wasting his time. At 5 feet 4 inches and thin, I was undersized. I also wasn't very fast and couldn't jump that well. Other than that, I had it all going on. Most of my game was heart and as much of that as I had, it wasn't enough to compensate for all my shortcomings; not at IU anyway.

The whole conversation took maybe 10 minutes and we never left the lobby, never sat down. At the end, he mentioned something about trying out if I still felt strongly about it. I thanked him for his time and honesty, hard as it was to take. Then I hopped in the van and the first words out of my mouth were: "I cannot do it. I can't go here."

I knew where I was going: home to Carmel and then to East Lansing, Michigan.

All that uncertainty disappeared, which in some ways made the quiet drive home a lot easier than the drive down. I was relieved. It was certain now that I needed to move on; leave IU in the rear view mirror and pursue my prospects at Michigan State.

That night, I got together with three high school teammates. Rosio was a freshman at Purdue, playing club soccer there; OB was going to play at Ball State; and Matt was going to take the pitch at Wabash College. They knew how much of a long shot it was for me to think I could play at IU, and they were all really curious about how the meeting went. We talked about it for a while, went to dinner, and talked about it some more, and I remember all of us agreeing after our talk that yeah, Michigan State was the right fit for me, the best choice. I went to bed certain of it.

I woke up the next morning thinking the exact opposite.

I can't explain it, except to say that this overpowering force deep in my gut was pushing me. It would not be denied, and I was starting to get sick about it.

My mom was ironing shirts that morning when I shuffled in the den and told her I still wanted to play at IU. I could tell my mom anything. She's one of the most thoughtful, empathetic listeners and counselors I know.

"Are you nuts?" she said. "What the heck are you talking about? We just drove there and back yesterday and you were done with the whole thing. Coach Yeagley told you that you'd never make it. You're not registered for classes. You don't have a place to live."

"I know," I sighed. "I know."

We stood there silent, looking at each other. The iron spurted a little steam.

"OK," my mom said. "Well, let's just think about it and see."

We didn't tell my dad. I just couldn't visualize that. He knew nothing of my doubts. As far as he was concerned, everything had fallen into place perfectly, and it had. My dad, more than anybody else I know, loves when things come together just so. He's a very disciplined thinker and precision-perfect planner. Can drive you nuts. I knew that if I backed out of MSU, I would flip the whole perfect table setting over and make a mess of things. I was not ready to propose that to my dad.

In a way, that anxiety worked to my advantage. I channeled all of it into my training regimen, hoping that by beating myself to death, I'd pound out or sweat out any crazy thoughts of trying to play soccer on a team I had no business considering. At the same time, I knew that a guy like me needed to train like a beast to be in peak physical condition to compete at the college level, wherever I played. So, every day for the next couple of months, I worked hard. By August, I was in great shape.

Except that the stronger I got, the stronger that little IU voice got, and the stronger that vision became. I kept ignoring the voice, erasing that image of me taking the field in my Indiana soccer uniform every time it surfaced in my mind, pushing deep any desire to play at Indiana, willing it to die.

I was going to wear green and white, be a Spartan, a legacy in the proud Kapsalis line started by my big brother. I was going to make my dad proud; going to re-connect with my high school buddies in Michigan. It was all set.

But that blasted voice; it wouldn't let me be.

Dan laid the groundwork for my dream.

2

CHAPTER

I've always tried to be a role model to children. The decision to go to IU afforded me that opportunity before ever stepping onto the field.

GOING SOUTH INSTEAD OF NORTH

CHAPTER 2:

GOING SOUTH INSTEAD OF NORTH

All these years later, I still shake my head and smile a little about how it happened.

It was August 12, 1983. I'll always remember the date. We were sitting around the dining room table—my parents, my brother Dean, my sister Deanne, and me—enjoying my last home-cooked meal for a while. The next morning, my mom and dad and I were driving up to East Lansing, Michigan, and I was going to start my college soccer career at Michigan State. Pete had finished playing there the previous fall, and Danny was already on the Indiana University campus for pre-season, two-a-day practices to start his junior year.

My mom's a great cook, and she pulled out all the stops—spaghetti, chicken, fresh bread, salad, the works. It was a big deal. Everybody was really excited for me to play college soccer at a great school. All of it made me fired up, except that I was having trouble eating. This churning inside me wouldn't stop, and I knew what it was. I had the IU Soccer Virus.

I can't explain it entirely. Who really can explain these things? As I sat there at the table, moving around the food on my plate, thoughts of Indiana University soccer were flowing and whirling in my head, filling it up. There wasn't room for anything else. I started thinking again about that time over the winter when I was at the mall and saw the replay of Indiana's national championship win over Duke.

I tried to shake myself back to reality, back to the moment at the dining room table. I forced myself to think about what an opportunity I had at Michigan State, following Pete's path, playing at a Big 10 school.

But, as much as I tried to persuade myself, I knew Michigan State soccer was not anything like Indiana soccer. It just wasn't. I loved the Spartans and they would continue improving, even winning a Big 10 Championship in 2008. But in the late 1970s and early 1980s, they were above average at best. In the same span, IU had won 106 games, lost 12, tied 4, won 1 national championship, and lost in national championship games twice.

I'm sitting there, already verbally committed to State, and I'm telling myself, *Who am I kidding with these thoughts about playing for IU? I'd never play there, never even make the team.* I knew that sure as my name is Paul and my hair is white. Coach Yeagley told me as much a few weeks earlier. It couldn't be any clearer if he'd have written it on my forearm in red ink.

But there was the what-if question, the hardest one for me to dismiss. Sitting at the dining room table, it popped up again. I couldn't think clearly. It was driving me nuts.

"So, are you all packed and ready to go tomorrow morning?" my dad finally asked. "We gotta head out at 8 o'clock so we meet the coach on time."

I hesitated, staring down at my plate.

"Whitey?"

I looked up and turned to my dad.

"I've been thinking, dad."

"Yeah," he said. "What is it?"

I couldn't believe this. *I'm crazy.* I thought. *What am I doing?* I couldn't get the words out.

"Whitey?" he said. "What is it, son?"

"I want to go to IU," I said barely above a whisper.

Silence.

"What?"

I said it again, my voice a little shaky.

"You wanna go to IU?" my dad said.

"Yeah," I said, "I want to try and play there."

"What are you telling me? When did all this come about?"

Now it was my time to be silent. I didn't know where to begin. All this stuff was spinning in my mind.

Both my parents stared at each other then my dad turned back to me with an expression that wasn't quite outrage but pretty close to it. Let's just call it shock.

I cleared my throat.

"I want to play soccer at IU."

I could see him reeling, trying his best to remain calm and process what he'd just heard; my mom, too. She'd known I'd had my doubts and that they were serious but she didn't know I'd made up my mind to act on my delusion. They were stunned, even looked a little dizzy, and I shouldn't have been surprised at that. I'd just dropped a bomb on them, and my timing couldn't have been worse.

My dad repositioned himself in the chair a little, trying to recalibrate his thinking, trying to figure out what to say. He took a deep breath, letting the air out slowly.

"Are you sure?" he finally said in a soft voice. "I mean, have you been thinking about it?"

"Dad," I said, almost chuckling. "It's about all I've been thinking for the last four months, night and day."

He paused, sizing me up, looking at me almost as if he was trying to figure out if I was bluffing him, playing a joke. He saw pretty quick that I wasn't. Over the next two hours, we had a soul-scouring discussion. I told them that every night since I had come home from my recruiting trip to MSU, I couldn't fall asleep without thinking, *Am I passing up a dream to play for IU and will I wonder the rest of my life whether I could have made the team?* I told them that as much as I tried to dismiss it, to bury it, the question kept coming back. I knew I'd have a rewarding career at Michigan State, I told them, and following Pete would be an honor. And, yeah, I have the partial scholarship, and yeah, Michigan State is a great school. But what if...? What if it just so happens that I am good enough to play for IU? What if I worked my ass off, got in the best shape of my life and actually was able to play for the greatest collegiate soccer program in the nation? What if that question never went away—and I knew it wouldn't now—even after I played at Michigan State? What if I was sitting in some dead-end job at the age of 40, anxious and aggravated with my life, all for squandering this one chance I had to pursue this wild dream? The answer is simple.

"I'd rather fail at IU," I told my mom and dad, "then spend the rest of my life wondering whether I could have made it."

It took a while to convince them, and who could blame them? This was nearly insane—throwing away a sure thing at the last minute to try for an unreachable goal, especially after the coach told me I wouldn't make the team. Sounds like the definition of crazy to me.

They had lots of questions, the first of which was what if I don't make the team at IU? What if I don't like the experience there? Then, they pointed out that I hadn't registered for classes and didn't have housing. We'd have to take care of all that now, a few days before classes start.

I just kept saying I've got to try. I've got to try, and I need to try this now in my life. I won't be in this spot again, ever.

Slowly, they came around. I think after understanding that I had wrestled with this for months, that I'd tried to dismantle the dream with logic, it just wasn't working and never would. I think back now on that moment and wonder what I would have done in their position, and I marvel at the patience, trust, and foresight my parents displayed. It was a beautiful lesson in parenting.

No matter what they were thinking, I believe they saw just how powerful this dream was and they didn't want to snuff it out.

For that perspective, I am eternally grateful, because, in that one moment, they showed me an enormous amount about what it means to be a parent, to give your kids the extraordinary lesson of pursuing dreams, as laughable as they may seem. You see, when you're allowed to chase a dream, the lessons you learn—whether or not you realize that dream—are invaluable. Maybe— probably—my parents thought I was nuts; and I was. But they saw the importance of allowing me to try.

They took a deep breath, swallowed hard, and said yes.

"Okay," my dad said, "but if that's the case, the first thing you're going to do tomorrow morning is get on the phone with the coach and tell him you've changed your mind. He's counting on you, and I hate to disappoint him. You made the decision. You've got to be the man to tell him. You're accountable."

I gulped, starting to realize what I was about to set in motion.

The next day, I woke up early from a restless night's sleep and finally worked up the nerve to call MSU Coach Joe Baum at 8 in the morning. I dialed him directly at his office and, much to my surprise, he answered the phone. Talk about an awkward phone conversation. He was shocked, understandably so, but he also was very professional.

I don't remember much about the conversation, except that it was very brief—maybe two minutes, thank God—and that Coach Baum said something about when I failed at IU; not if, but when I failed, he'd have a spot for me at MSU.

After hanging up, I immediately felt that I'd made a mistake. Considering options is a lot easier than making and living with the actual decision. I knew I had given this one a great deal of thought, but once I had made that final decision and brought closure with the phone call to Coach Baum, I experienced another rush of emotions. I felt that I'd gone back on my word and it literally made me sick to my stomach telling him. Then, there was that other, undeniable feeling: fear. *What was I getting myself into? This little dream I'd whipped up looked pretty foolhardy now, didn't it?* How does the old saying go? You've made your bed; now you've got to sleep in it. Well, I'd made this decision and now I'd have to live with it, whatever may come, and I wasn't particularly optimistic at that point.

I had some scrambling to do. The next call was to Coach Yeagley at IU. When the phone was passed to him, he immediately said, "Hi Whitey," and the fact that he greeted me by name made me feel at least a little encouraged. Or maybe I was so desperately looking for a shred of hope that I seized on that. When I told him what I was planning, Coach Yeagley was almost as stunned as Coach Baum, and certainly perplexed. But, he, too, was very professional. He also was brief, passing me to one of the assistant coaches, who explained the tryout process. I'd known a little about it from Danny during the year the Hoosiers won the national championship, the season that had such a magical effect on me. The assistant said he would be in touch with more details about the walk-on process. Two days later, I received an envelope from IU Soccer, and I felt a little charge crackle through me. Inside were medical release forms, tryout dates and times, that sort of stuff. A couple days after that, I was packed and riding in the family van with my mom to Bloomington. Instead of heading north to East Lansing, I was heading south, and I tried not to think too much about the analogy.

When we arrived, I registered for classes and then realized that I'd forgotten a somewhat important detail my parents mentioned in our dinner talk the night before I was supposed to leave for Michigan State: I had no place to live. I'd been accepted academically to IU but, because I was sure that I'd be attending Michigan State, I never pursued housing. Now, here I was, all my clothes and basic living necessities in the van, with no place to unpack.

After some negotiating and running around, we found the housing office and the ladies there set me up in a lounge in Reed Residence Hall. Now, I don't know how many of you have lived in a lounge, but let me say that it's a rare experience in personal exposure. You have a dresser, a couch and, in my case, you live at the end of a hallway. Visualize yourself residing in the lobby of a chain hotel and you'll start to get the picture. People stroll right through at all hours of the day and night. It's noisy, and you feel a little like you're part of some weird public art exhibit, like a living, breathing statue in the museum, or a mannequin in a store window display of dilapidated furniture. In other words, it sucked mightily.

Welcome to my dream world, I thought. *More like a nightmare.*

I took one look and told my mom I'd changed my mind. I wasn't coming to IU.

"Don't get so antsy," she said. "Give things some time. Everything has a way of working out just fine."

I guess deep down inside, I knew I really didn't have a choice. If I was going to try to play soccer at IU, I had to do what I had to do; had to endure a lot of unexpected bumps in the road. If I finally was going to answer that what-if question, I needed to live in a lounge. So, I moved in and waited for a real dorm room to open somewhere on campus. They told me it might take a month or two, and I felt my heart sink, especially because Reed was a 30-minute walk from the athletic facilities and the dorms where the soccer players lived.

I must have looked pretty pathetic because after a couple of days, Danny offered me the floor of his apartment. The place was full— Danny had two roommates—but he said I could put my bags on the floor of the living room and sleep in the dining room. When something more permanent came up in the dorms, I could move. But for now, Danny said, I could have the floor. So, I packed my stuff, found a sleeping bag, and moved up from the hotel lobby to the dining room—hey, at least it wasn't the bathroom—and I was grateful.

That was one of those small developments that occurred through the generosity of someone, in this case, my brother, that would lead to something immensely important. And, it makes me think now about how you never know what impact your generosity will have on someone, what ripple effect will occur if you extend a hand, or if you don't. I soon found out how I would benefit from Danny's gesture of generosity, and it would change the course of my sorry prospects in a big way.

Danny lived in Dunnhill apartments, the place, it turned out, where a bunch of IU soccer players lived. So, in many ways, it was precisely the environment I wanted, a place where I could be around the guys, where at least they might recognize my face, and a place that also was about two blocks from the athletic fields.

Although all the returning and newly recruited players had begun practicing at IU, tryouts for me were weeks away. And, being on campus early, I had some time on my hands. So, I'd get up, walk over to a church parking lot behind and above Bill Armstrong Stadium, where the soccer team played and practiced, and watch two-a-day practices through a chain-link fence. I went up there for 10 consecutive days and watched, and what I saw scared me, frankly.

I saw 34 guys on the field being led through their paces by a team of coaches that weren't messing around. Thirty-four very strong, very fast, very competitive soccer players on the best collegiate soccer team in the U.S., the defending national champs, practicing more intensely than I'd seen any team anywhere practice. I started having those doubts again. Big time. Everyone back home, except for my family, was sure I'd never make it at IU, and I was beginning to think they were right.

But, it was helpful to see what I was shooting for, what level I'd be expected to play at, to mentally prepare for tryouts. And, the more I watched, the more one thought sunk into my head: *You know, I could see myself on this field.* In retrospect, I was a little naïve. I was watching from a few hundred yards away, sort of like watching pro sports on TV. You're thinking, *How in God's green acres could that guy have missed that play? What a bonehead! I could have done better than that.* And then you realize that the speed, power, and pressure of the game on the ground would make a normal human being's head spin, and that the normal human being probably would get his head knocked off his shoulders. Up close, I was to discover, the ball and the players move a lot faster. Those guys in the red, white, and gray practice gear were a lot stronger and more competitive than I knew. In this case, though, my naiveté was a healthy thing. If I'd known precisely what I was getting myself into, I probably never would have driven down to Bloomington.

Most days after watching practices, I'd go for long runs and work out on my own. I wanted to be as ready as humanly possible for that pressure-packed, soul-crushing ordeal of tryouts. One day after a workout, I was wandering around the apartment complex and bumped into Pat McGauley, an All-American soccer player at IU who was entering his final season. I knew Pat from a soccer clinic he participated in up in Indianapolis about three years earlier. By that time, with all the soccer in her life, my mom—ever the shrewd, resourceful thinker—decided to embrace the sport. She opened a soccer store that became very successful. One summer, she set up a soccer clinic for about 300 kids. Pat, three other IU players, and an assistant coach drove in to lead the sessions. It was really cool. I was a high school sophomore then and Pat was one of the premier college soccer players in the U.S., vying for a spot on the national team. At some point during the clinic, I'd gotten introduced to him and it was a huge deal for me.

So, I remembered Pat, and when I bumped into him while he was getting the mail that afternoon at Dunnhill, I said hi and reintroduced myself. He didn't remember me—who would?—but he was really cool. Pat always was a very nice guy. He shook my hand, and we started talking and he asked what I was doing down there. I told him I was planning on trying out for the team.

"Cool," he said. "Where are you living?"

"I don't really have a place," I said. "Right now, I'm sleeping on the floor in Danny's apartment."

A surprised expression spread across Pat's face.

"That's amazing," he said. "A couple of guys on the team were expecting a third roommate to come back but he isn't."

Those two guys were All-American soccer players John Stollmeyer and Keith Meyer, and they just happened to be a couple of my soccer idols. The summer before, Indianapolis hosted this sports festival, a sort of mini-Olympics for athletes in the U.S. Participants from four regions of the country converged on the city over about two weeks and played games in a tournament format. Each sport featured the best college—and some high school—athletes in the country representing their region. I was following the soccer and watched these two guys from IU—John Stollmeyer and Keith Meyer—and I thought, *My God, I'd love to be them, to be as good as they are.* It was amazing. Out of that entire tournament, those two guys drew almost my entire focus.

And now, they needed a roommate. I felt my heart race but I didn't know what to say. Thank God Pat did.

"Listen, I'd like to introduce you to them," he told me. "Maybe you could live with them and it would work out for all you guys. They're looking for a roommate. You need a place to stay and who knows? Maybe it'll help you with making the team and all that."

I was really nervous. Couldn't believe it. Here I was this awkward, humble freshman chasing a naïve dream and I was about to come face-to-face with a couple of guys who personified that dream. If everything went well, I'd be their roommate. I was almost shaking at the prospect.

Pat took me up to their apartment a few minutes later, introduced me, and I could tell right away their very distinct personalities. Keith was from St. Louis and, coming out of high school a couple years earlier, was the national high school player of the year. Handsome—I'd later find out that all ladies were crazy about him, but that he was serious with a girl from back home who he'd eventually marry—Keith was tall and lean, the kind of guy who wore pressed khakis and polos. In general, I could sense he was pretty reserved, all business, and a little suspicious of me. He also wasn't real interested in making a new friend, let alone having a new roommate, and I could appreciate that. What surprised both of us was how much that would change and how quickly.

And John? Well, John "Stolly" Stollmeyer was an altogether different animal. He was probably an inch or two shorter than Keith and all thick muscle, carved from stone. He'd arrived at IU from Virginia because of Keith. The two of them played on a U.S. national team in Australia and Keith persuaded Stolly, who was being chased by every major collegiate soccer program in the nation, to come to Indiana. Stolly enrolled and started as a mid-fielder next to his buddy Keith. They would remain starters, roommates, and close friends at IU for the next three years.

As I got to know them, that pairing always struck me as funny, almost like the old play, movie, and TV show, *The Odd Couple*. Keith was groomed, meticulous, and reserved. Stolly was scruffy, a dreamer with a high-energy, outgoing, outspoken personality that some perceived as a little rough around the edges, even abrasive. But he had a big heart, a really big heart, and loved to laugh. He was a genuinely friendly, unpretentious person. I had no idea then just how sincere a guy he would turn out to be or how close he and I would become.

Standing there in the apartment, they looked me up and down. Then the interrogation started and went something like this:

"Can you pay rent?" Keith asked.

"Yeah," I said.

"You're in," Stolly said, smiling. He shook my hand, slapped me on the back. "Why don't you go ahead and get your stuff, move in, and we'll see how it goes this year."

And that was it. Stolly and I shared a room, the optimal arrangement for all parties involved. He took me grocery shopping for the first time, showed me how to do laundry, and gave me the lay of the land in the apartment.

"We've got pretty simple rules around here, Whitey," he told me. "Don't cause any problems and pay rent on time."

I could handle that.

Call it Divine Intervention — I might call it Daniel Intervention — but that stroke of luck was one of the most significant breaks I got at IU. It's what one of my aunts likes to call an "amazing grace" moment. And, when I look back on how it all came together — so happenstance — it makes me stop in wonderment. My brother making room for me at his apartment allowed me to bump into somebody at the mailbox who I'd met in passing three years earlier, and that chance encounter opened the door to living with two of my idols who, oddly enough, needed me and ended up helping me immensely. It was crazy. It was amazing grace.

I moved in and it went pretty well. I was really respectful and wary of overstepping my place, and both guys were friendly, solid roommates. They had separate but useful takes on my plan to try out for the soccer team. Stolly's take was, hey, work hard and go for it. You've got nothing to lose. Nothing ventured; nothing gained. Keith was a little less enthusiastic. He thought I was wasting my time. To him — and I really valued his observations, believe it or not, because

they were honest and helped me understand just what I was facing—
it seemed almost impossible that I would ever make a contribution
to the team, even if I made the roster. After a couple of weeks, while
I obsessed over my chances and stalked practices, Stolly and Keith
wished me well and went on the team's first road trip out east for a
three-day, two-game spin.

The three days of tryouts started while the team was gone. On the
first morning, I was a mental mess. Tryouts didn't start until 3:30
p.m. So, apart from the sleepless night before, I had all day to think
about it, which is pretty much how I spent the time. *Can I do this?
Am I good enough to make the team? Should I have stayed with
MSU? What have I done?* It was an agonizing six or seven hours, but
I think I found at least some peace knowing that I was going to find
out pretty quick just how realistic this dream was.

I got dressed in my soccer gear—shorts, t-shirt, shin guards, socks,
and cleats—at the apartment, and I remember walking uphill to the
practice fields next to Bill Armstrong Stadium. I was twitchy and
anxious and pretty uncertain—as nervous as I have ever been in my
life—but I also felt as ready as I ever would be. I'd been training
hard for weeks—been playing 13 years, really—for this chance.

When I stepped onto the soccer field that day, I was surrounded by
about 20 guys. The odds were ridiculous. Coaches may take one of
us, but there were no guarantees anybody would make it. In fact,
chances were greater that every last one of us would go through
three days of hellacious drills, then get a pat on the back and be
brushed aside like lint on a lapel.

Assistant coaches coordinated the tryouts, and I soon discovered
that the range of talent was vast. Many of the guys had been training

as hard as I'd been. But some just plain didn't have the skills to be on this field. After a while, it became apparent that about seven had been top-notch high school players, every bit as strong as I was—stronger in some areas—and that ratcheted up my nerves.

You never know what to expect at any tryout, and it was safe to say that I had no idea how grueling this one would be. For starters, the weather was extremely hot and muggy—classic south central Indiana conditions for that time of year—which made me glad I'd worked out as hard as I had. I needed every ounce of energy just to hang in there.

And then there were the mini scrimmages. Coaches would place goals 30 yards apart, facing each other, then throw two of us out there for three-minute games. The guy who scored the most goals won. After each game, we'd rest for three minutes then jump back in for another round against a different opponent. It progressed to 2 versus 2, then 3 versus 3, and it was exhausting, the most intense competition I've experienced on the soccer field; so intense, in fact, that everybody got a little chippy. Tempers flared, guys shoved each other and a couple of scuffles almost broke out. The setup didn't exactly play to my strengths, either, which always have been focused on team—not individual—success. I didn't win as many bouts as I wanted and that made me more nervous. But, I hung in there every second and just kept working and playing my game.

Through all the tryouts I'd endured over the years, I'd always been able to get a pretty clear idea of where I stood after an hour or so, and where I had stood always had been in the upper tier of talent. Not now. Any confidence I'd had was sweated out of me. Too many of those top players at the tryout were too good. I couldn't tell how I stacked up, whether I was playing well or what the coaches thought.

That anxiety, that uncertainty, was the most agonizing part, although it also made me push myself harder than I'd ever done and reach down deep for effort I didn't think I had. I was so focused on doing the absolute best I could, I was almost oblivious to anyone around me.

After the most intense two days of soccer in my life, I felt that I'd held my own, but deep down, I really couldn't be sure. On that third day, the IU team had returned from the road trip and was practicing on another portion of the field. Coach Yeagley, the man who would make the decision on whether to keep any of us scruffy wanna-bees, was with the real team, out of our sight. At the very end of that final day, with about a half-hour left in tryouts, he came over and watched.

I'd made up my mind about one thing during those three days: I was not going to be cut from the IU soccer team for lack of effort. And, on that final day, I knew that, with Coach Yeagley silently scrutinizing those last few minutes of tryouts, it was an all-or-nothing-moment. I didn't care how foolish I might have looked—something else that would come in quite handy later in my soccer journey. I gave it everything I had. And then I gave some more.

It was one very extreme half-hour of soccer—maybe the hardest I've worked for 30 minutes—followed by probably the most nerve-wracking 15 minutes of my life while the coaches deliberated. It started with a surprise vote. Coach Yeagley passed out pencils and little sheets of paper and asked each of us to write down the name of the guy, excluding ourselves, we thought should make the team. After that, he and two assistants went into a meeting. As exhausted as I was, as drenched in sweat as I was, I could barely stand still. When the three of them emerged, Coach Yeagley thanked everyone for their effort.

"We're going to keep one guy this year, fellas," he said, and for an instant, I felt stillness fill the space around me. And then he said it. "Whitey Kapsalis, you've made the IU soccer team."

Chills swept over me, and I felt like I was floating. It was the most incredible sensation in the world. A couple guys came up and congratulated me but so many thoughts overloaded my mind, I'm not sure how I responded. I was sort of dazed, thrilled beyond explanation, relieved, more exhausted than I'd ever been. I literally could not believe it was happening to me. I thought about how I'd turned down the sure thing at Michigan State. I thought about close friends of mine and parents of high school teammates telling me, "What in the world are you doing? You're never going to make it." I thought about all those times over the past few weeks that I couldn't sleep then woke up in the morning doubting, being scared really.

And, it's a funny thing. Even when I was experiencing all that, I never got angry at the doubters. I can't exactly explain why. I guess I could appreciate how the situation must have looked to them, and I think I felt like they were saying what they said as a way of looking out for my best interests; because they cared about me. And, you know what? I was grateful for that concern. I know. I know. I'm a naïve guy.

However you slice it, here I was. I was going to wear the cream and crimson of the best college soccer team in the country. I was an IU Hoosier soccer player. Hot diggedy dog.

Not everyone shared my same level of enthusiasm.

"Congratulations," Coach Yeagley said after the tryout players drifted off. He sounded about as excited as a waitress telling a cook to include fries with that burger. "We're going to red-shirt you. See you tomorrow at practice. Three thirty." Then he and the other coaches turned and went back to work with the team.

Red-shirt? I had no idea what he was talking about. Did they designate half the team red and the other half white? I sort of shrugged it off and told myself I'd leave that for later. For now, I could take a minute to enjoy the moment. I'd made the team. I had to repeat it in my mind, almost say it aloud. *I'd made the team.*

I ran back to the apartment and called home. My mom answered and I swear she broke into a Greek tribal celebration dance. She was goofy excited and called my dad at work. He called me and he was just as goofy excited. He followed that up with a letter to me, sent that day, on business letterhead that had "Reach for the Stars" streaming across the top. My dad is a big letter writer, and when I got the letter a few days later, I got choked up with emotion. They knew how much making the team meant to me and told me how much they admired my guts, sacrifice, and passion to pull this off.

Stolly and Keith arrived at the apartment, and they might have thought I was in need of medication. There I was, a guy who had barely made the team, but I was beaming. They both congratulated me; Stolly a little more emphatically than Keith. Stolly was genuinely excited. To Keith, my making the team was an afterthought. But neither of them said much, and for good reason. They were pretty focused on the upcoming season, when the team had a real shot at a second consecutive national championship.

As exhausting as the day had been, I had a tough time falling asleep that night. I remember lying in bed and being overwhelmed with joy and pride at proving something that even I had serious doubts about. I might have been naïve, but I realized that moments like the one I was experiencing that day are pretty rare, and I couldn't help relishing all of it for an hour or so after my head hit the pillow. *Dang, I did it. I actually made the team.*

The next day the sunrise was a bright one, which was appropriate, I guess. I was about to get a very rude awakening and start on what would be the most challenging journey of my life.

Keith Meyer played in 4 Final Fours and was a leader by example.

3

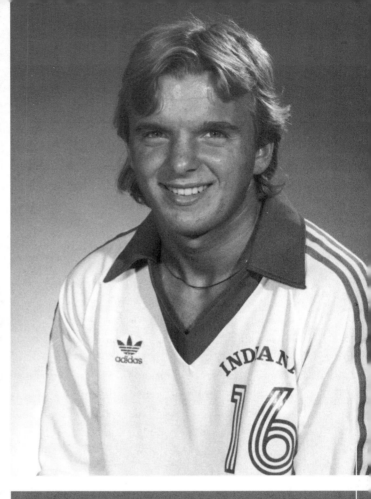

I wore Stolly's jersey #16 for this photo, but was just happy to be a part of IU Soccer.

HUMILITY

CHAPTER 3:

HUMILITY

Red-shirting, I discovered on my first day of practice, is a National Collegiate Athletic Association (NCAA) status in which the athlete technically is part of the team but is prohibited from playing in games for that team for a full year. Most times, a player is red-shirted to give him or her an extra year to develop by getting all that work in practice. At the end of the year, typically the athlete's first on campus, the player does not lose eligibility for that red-shirt year but has improved his or her skills substantially.

That's the technical definition of red shirt. But, like everyone knows, the difference between technical definitions of things and actually living them can be pretty distinct. Living the red-shirt experience is very much like being in limbo, and let me tell you, soccer limbo is not a scenic place. I know. Lord, do I know.

I'm not sure what I believed when the coaches made me a redshirt. I might have thought—again, naïvely—that they saw a spark of talent buried deep within me that just might rise to the surface if I had a year of rigorous practice with a team of elite players. Now, with the wisdom of experience on my side, I see things in a slightly less rosy context. Basically, I think they kept me because I was a nice kid with marginal soccer skills who happened to be from Indiana. Or, they thought that a year of red-shirting would make me see the futility of my expectations and lead me to quit.

Either way, there I was—barely the 35th guy on a 35-man team, which basically placed me one step above a manager. At practices,

I was one of about 10 guys who are subs on the non-starters' squad. Talk about being low on the food chain. Some days I wouldn't even get a chance to play in practice scrimmages. I was, in sports parlance, a practice dummy, practice meat.

I don't think I ever had to pass out towels or water, but I got really good at moving goals, retrieving soccer balls, and performing other grunt and "go-fer" work, as in "Go for this, Whitey. Go for that, Whitey."

I also got really good at being humble. Not that I ever was the loud, boastful type, but if I had been, the red-shirt experience would have pounded it out of me.

The most difficult part was working so hard day in and day out and not knowing if I was making progress. I wasn't part of anybody's plans. My name never was mentioned during strategy discussions about upcoming games. Heck, the coaches barely knew my name. It was completely different from my high school experience, where I'd be talked about all the time, where I might lead those discussions.

NCAA rules also prohibited me from sitting on the bench during games and, of course, I never traveled with the team. So, I never even got a uniform. My high school buddies would come to watch a game, and I'd have to tell them I wasn't suiting up, wasn't even going to be on the sidelines. We'd climb the stairs and sit in the stadium just like the rest of the fans. Not exactly what I would have experienced at Michigan State.

Same with my parents. They would drive down to Bloomington and sit with me in the bleachers and, at some point the inevitable, painful question would come up in one form or another: Are you ever going to play? I would say, I think I so.

After a few game-viewing experiences like that, I started wondering whether they believed I'd actually made the team. So, I'd walk them near the locker room before and after games, making sure I'd see some of my teammates and give them a hearty wave, maybe a clap on the back, wish them good luck. Sometimes, I'd even walk in the locker room for a minute while my mom and dad were around on game days. Thank God, all the guys would respond and acknowledge me by name.

See, I almost felt like saying to my folks, *I'm on the team. How else would they know my name? How could I go into the locker room?*

All of it definitely hurts your pride and saps your confidence.

But, at the same time, I was proud knowing that I was one of 35 guys on this premier team, the best team in the country. I had to tell myself that there were probably 50,000, maybe 500,000 kids who would give their left eye to be part of the IU soccer program.

I never felt IU owed me anything. The coaches gave me a chance—however remote—and it was up to me to take it from there. I tried to stay focused on that mindset, and it helped. I also think I learned something that I already was doing subconsciously— that staying optimistic and encouraged is an active, conscious, ongoing effort. You have to work at it, just like you have to work at improving your dribbling skills or passing or endurance, every day.

And, I felt at least that year, I had time. I told myself I was in it for the long haul, which also helped my frame of mind. So, I just kept grinding away, looking to make an impression.

Living close to the soccer fields was a huge benefit, if for no other reason than it made my walk to practice about five minutes instead of the half hour it took to schlep between the fields and Reed dorm. If I'd have come home to the dorm where regular students were living, I'd be tempted to hang out a lot more, lose my focus. Guys would be telling me to play intramural soccer where I could have more fun. People would be saying, "Hey, there's a party at the SAE House tonight. Why don't you forget about soccer for a while and cut loose?" In other words, it would have been so easy to give up on the dream if I was living in Reed. And, I didn't want to give up on the dream, at least not yet.

I started to see that I had another advantage; two, really. Their names were Keith and Stolly. They weren't All-American soccer players for nothing. Living with them helped me immeasurably. In short, Keith and Stolly were great role models.

In practice, they set an extremely high bar for work ethic, which made a strong impression, even if I didn't scrimmage against them, which I didn't very often. After practice or class or a trip to the library, instead of heading back to a dorm, I'd come back and they'd be talking soccer. Some nights, it would be general stuff and insights about the game and players. Other nights, they'd go through specific strategies. How are we going to beat Clemson next week? How we are going to prepare for Evansville's physical style of play? They'd talk about different roles and expectations for themselves and their teammates depending on certain scenarios. The passion and preparation they showed for striving to be the best was so powerful then and to this day. While they talked, I kept my mouth shut and ears open—a great way to learn, especially from those two guys.

Over the months, our relationship strengthened, and I could see I played a key role. Stolly and Keith, their personalities being what they were, had a tendency to drive each other nuts. Stolly was all spontaneity. Keith was calculating. Stolly would always, always, tell me to go for my soccer dream. Keith was much more cautious, thoughtful. Stolly would cram for tests and class projects a day or two in advance. Keith would grind away for weeks on each assignment, study religiously every night.

As nutty as it could be at times, as often as I wondered how these two distinct personalities made it work, I think living with Keith and Stolly provided me with a near-perfect balance, and I landed somewhere in the middle of both guys' life views. I think I provided a little buffer in the world that was our apartment, although I probably leaned a little more toward Stolly's approach to life. What can I say? I'm a dreamer.

The typical example would arise when we had some rare free time, when the relentlessness of soccer and academics eased up a little and we could squeeze in some fun.

"Hey Whitey," Stolly would say. "What're you doing?"

"I don't know. Nothing really. Got a test tomorrow."

"Worry about your test then. Let's go. I got something you gotta' do."

Interested, of course—I was always interested in what Stolly was cooking up—I'd ask what he had in mind.

"Man, we gotta have a pizza at Nick's."

I was all in. "Sounds good," I'd say.
   Somehow or other, even though he was studying in his room, Keith would hear our plan.

"Hey, Whitey," he'd shout. "Don't you have a test tomorrow? Stolly? Doesn't Whitey have a test tomorrow?"

I'd freeze but a little smile would start to spread on my face, the little brother caught conspiring with the mischievous middle brother by the responsible oldest brother. Part of that smile sprung from the knowledge that Keith cared — really cared — enough to make sure I was staying on track.

"Well, yeah, I do," I'd say. "But we're only going out for a little while."

Stolly would chime in.

"Yeah, he's fine, Keith. He's fine. He's all set." Stolly would wink at me. "Totally prepared."

And, as we headed for the door, we'd hear Keith shout, "Okay, but hey, I'm just saying. It's about your education."

I don't want to paint a portrait of Keith that would lead anyone to perceive him as cold. He truly cared for me and would show it all the time. When the three of us would go out to a party, Stolly and I would jump right in, wanting to get to know everyone in the room. Keith could mingle with anyone, a very smooth conversationalist, but he'd be more inclined to stand back and watch me. I think he got a real kick out of my outgoing personality. And, a lot of times, if I was out later than he was — which happened more often than not — I'd come walking in the apartment, and he'd call out to me from his room.

Keith had a rocking chair next to his bed. He'd start talking with me then point to the chair and say, "Have a seat. How was your night?"

That was our catch up time, and he started it right away my freshman year. I think it was his way of keeping tabs on me, looking after me, and I loved it. I loved it so much, in fact, that he'd sometimes fall asleep, and I'd just keep right on talking.

It didn't always go so smoothly, though. One night my freshman year, I came home with another close friend of mine from the soccer team, Mike "Mickey" McCartney, and I got a little loud. Keith told me to quiet down, but I wasn't in the mood for quieting down. I was in the mood for laughing and talking—way too loud—with Mickey; listening to some tunes. Keith could close the door if he wanted more quiet. Besides, it was a weekend.

Keith didn't quite see it my way, and he yelled at me. Now, Keith Meyer is a soft-spoken man who rarely loses his temper. So, when he says something, you listen. Or at least you should listen. That was the lesson freshman red-shirt Whitey Kapsalis was about to learn.

I went back to his room and we got to barking at each other and the next thing I know, we started shoving each other and a scuffle broke out. Luckily Mickey was there, jumped in and broke it up before it got too serious.

And, here's the funny thing about that little incident: It made Keith and me a whole lot closer, like real brothers. We grew a great deal that night, came to understand each other's perspective, respected each other a little more, and, more than anything else, appreciated the friendship and bond we had. We didn't want to lose each other. I actually think that rasslin' match was a healthy thing for us. We never had another argument.

Stolly and I, of course, had plenty of fun, and I don't really recall that we ever got into a serious scrape with one another. We'd kid around quite a bit and debate things, but always with sincere affection for each other.

And, we had our quiet moments, too, mostly late at night after studying at the kitchen table. It could be midnight or 1:00 in the morning, and Stolly would close the books and say, "Let's get out of here."

We'd throw on our jackets and walk through Indiana's beautiful campus. That was our thing, the times when we'd share quite a bit. He knew exactly where I was emotionally, and I think I was the guy he felt the safest with. If he was having some rough times, he'd tell me—almost always on those walks—and I'd do the same, and we'd keep it between us. Our trust was sacred and those walks really helped broaden my understanding of the human condition. At that young age, I was under the impression that a guy like Stolly— All-American soccer player on the best team in the country, a smart, good looking, outgoing, confident guy—had no problems whatsoever. But I was wrong. He had some of the same self-doubts and vulnerabilities that we all carry around with us. Apart from understanding that we all share more than we might realize, I was so grateful that I could kind of pay back his kindness toward me, that we had this good energy exchange. It wasn't all Stolly providing support to me. He could lean on me once in a while, and that forged a close, really strong bond.

All of this started coming together about halfway through my freshman year. We were roommates first and then, as I hung in there at practices, we became teammates. It's tough to say exactly when I was validated as their teammate, but I do remember late in the season getting a chance to scrimmage against the starters. I had a lot of energy and probably was a little pissed about being overlooked, a little desperate, too, and I channeled it all into my effort for that brief scrimmage. I guess it showed because I remember Keith and Stolly coming up to me individually and saying something like, "Wow, Whitey, you looked really good out there this afternoon. You might have something." It was the first time both of them seemed to think I belonged and, especially coming from Keith, that meant a great deal. Their acknowledgment of me as a soccer player was a tremendous boost to my confidence.

All of that helped ease the pain and humiliation of being a red-shirt freshman, but those didn't go away completely. Practices always were an endurance test physically and psychologically. Some days, I'd play five minutes in scrimmages. Some days, like I said, I wouldn't play at all. One time I'd play forward. The next I'm in the midfield.

It's an almost insurmountable mountain. No matter what, you go unnoticed as a redshirt. It's understandable conceptually. The coaches have a job to do—get those top 11 or 18 players ready to play their best soccer week in and week out. Even if you were a star in practice, you're prohibited from playing in real games as a red-shirt. Being one can and does end plenty of athletes' dreams.

I was extremely lucky. My family was incredibly supportive. My parents, even though I'd taken this lark on their dime, always propped me up emotionally. And then, there was Stolly, bless his heart. After my one, brief, glorious run in that scrimmage, I didn't have many more glorious moments. I barely had any chances to have more of those moments. I'd come home after a few days of practice hell, and Stolly could tell I was really dragging.

"Hey, I noticed that ball you played today," he'd say. "That was a good ball. You know, when you're defending, you ought to work on moving your feet a little bit more and being a little tougher." Sometimes, he'd even go as far as saying that I had a chance to contribute in a big way some day, that I should just stay with it.

To some people on some days, the words probably would sound ludicrous, patronizing. But to me, the little nuggets of encouragement Stolly, Keith, and my parents tossed my way were more precious than gold. They never let me get too far down in the doldrums. They helped me believe that I was OK, that this ordeal was going to turn out fine, no matter what. My roommates and my folks did that all the time for me and I will never be able to tell them how much it meant. Just a kind word every now and then can do wonders for somebody, can be the difference between success and failure, can be enough to keep a person hanging in there for another day. And, so much of life is about getting back up after being knocked on your ass and hanging in there for another day.

I benefited from the thoughtfulness of other people too, like Pat McGauley, who demonstrated his All-American stature to me routinely, especially with one gesture a few weeks into my red-shirt year.

Adidas, the sporting goods manufacturer, sponsors IU soccer, which means the company supplies all the team gear, and that gear is really cool, top-of-the-line equipment. Everybody on the team had a full complement—cleats, running shoes, shin guards, flip flops, warm-ups, roomy bag to carry all the stuff. You name it; it had an Adidas logo on it, looked pretty stylish, and was free to all players. Except me. I got a practice jersey, shorts, and socks and had to supply everything else. It was another little humiliation that wasn't personal, just an oversight that you have to endure when you're the red-shirt, 35th man on a 35-member team. It just didn't matter to most people.

Well, for whatever reason, it mattered to Pat McGauley, who had so many other things to deal with. A few weeks into the season, Pat noticed that I didn't have any of that stuff, walked over to Coach Yeagley's office, and told him. After the next practice, coach came up and told me to be sure to see the trainer to get my gear. I'd never gotten a free pair of shoes in my life, and for me to walk in, try on a couple of beautiful pairs of Adidas Copa Mundials and World Cups, and get the size that fit me just right was an incredibly important feeling; a small thing maybe, but one of those experiences that really made me feel like a part of the team. I had Pat to thank for that.

All those kind acts, encouraging words, and sensitivity to my lowly status were and are such powerful indicators of character. Apart from keeping me going, they provided me with wonderful role-modeling in a way that was very different from—but arguably more important than—learning to play my best soccer. They were lessons about caring for your fellow human beings, about the importance of taking a moment or two to show some kindness when you don't have to, when it probably doesn't matter to anyone but that individual who really needs it at that moment. Even if I failed in my dream, I'd remember these gestures and how much they meant to me when I was down and forgotten. And I knew one thing: I'd make darn sure that I was going to treat others in similar positions the way I was treated by those thoughtful people who boosted me up when I deeply needed it. To this day, that's a central part of who I am.

While my personal soccer exploits didn't exactly inspire shock and awe, the team was rolling along like a cream and crimson locomotive, gaining speed throughout the season. We lost the first game 2-1 at Penn State and then didn't lose another game the entire season, although we tied four times—against Duke, St. Louis University, Akron, and Alabama A & M. Once we got into the post-season NCAA tournament, the boys took care of business, beating Akron in overtime and St. Louis and Virginia before the final in Ft. Lauderdale, Florida on December 10.

As a redshirt, I wasn't going to be on that team flight, even in the luggage compartment. But my fellow teammate and buddy Mickey, who was injured, and I caught a flight and stayed in the team hotel for a few days—on our own dimes—to support the guys and be part of the whole experience. After all, it was the national championship game. You never know when that opportunity will arise again, and Mickey and I really wanted to absorb as much of it as possible.

NCAA rules prohibited us from participating in any team activities like practices, meetings, and dinners. So, we experienced the championship game against Columbia University in much the same way as fans would, in the bleachers. And, the experience was everything we could have hoped for. Pat McGauley scored in overtime on a great pass from freshman forward Rodrigo Castro, and we won 1-0. Mickey and I stormed the field with a bunch of other fans. It was wild. I couldn't have been more ecstatic for Pat, who had done so much for me and, really, for everyone on that team.

Indiana University had won another national championship for Hoosier soccer, the first back-to-back championships for the program. What made it extra exciting for me personally was that my brother Danny was on the team, although he didn't play in that particular game. The celebration back at the hotel was crazy, as you might imagine, and Stolly and Keith erased a lot of the sting of being a redshirt by going out of their way to make me feel like I was part of the team celebration and that I had contributed all year long. Again, it was an example of thoughtfulness that made such a powerful impression on me.

Back at campus, we were definitely the buzz in Bloomington for a few weeks. Lots of people gave us recognition and congratulations, especially students at parties or walking around campus. I distinctly remember the pride I felt knowing that I was on a national championship team. I'd see "IU Soccer National Champion" t-shirts for sale in the bookstore and spot students wearing them. Professors would congratulate us in front of the class, which would prompt everybody to give us a standing ovation—and, in a lecture hall, that could mean 300 people cheering for you. Later that year, we were introduced at halftime of a basketball game, and 17,000 people got so loud I thought the roof of the building would blow. To witness all the hard work of everybody paying off like that was almost indescribable. And, although I arguably was the smallest contributor to that team, there was no denying I contributed. That went a long way toward keeping me motivated.

But neither I nor anyone else with eyes and ears would ever mistake those celebrations for the one after IU won the basketball national championship in 1987. The soccer landscape at IU back then was part of the ongoing, tangled, rich, and frustrating story of soccer in the U.S.

College soccer had been around for 80 years—the first official intercollegiate game was played in 1904 between Harvard and Haverford College, although some set the first game as far back as a rugby-soccer match in 1876 between Princeton and Rutgers. Yet, outside of places like Indiana University, it always felt like the game was either on life support or about ready to explode in popularity. Weird.

The saga is well documented in a couple of books by the eloquent writer David Wangerin and in many articles. My simplified version of the whole thing can be distilled into a couple of critical points:

Soccer has endured a perennially lower status compared to gridiron football, and the game's overall popularity was complicated by a lack of national collegiate leadership and the inability of colleges and professional ranks to deal with the international influence of the game here.

What's a little curious to me was that at the time of that first official intercollegiate game, gridiron football was under siege on many college campuses for being too violent, dangerous, and altogether nonacademic. Sound familiar? Unfortunately for soccer fans, football had taken hold of the American psyche by the 1870s, especially on college campuses, where a number of rivalries had gotten people very fired up about school spirit and state pride. But soccer's biggest problem on college campuses may have been, as Wangerin writes, that "it lacked violence."

"In an industrialized country increasingly fearful of becoming effete," Wangerin writes in *Distant Corners: American Soccer's History of Missed Opportunities and Lost Causes* (2011, Temple University Press), "aggression on the gridiron, even at the risk of serious injury, had come to be perceived as a welcome demonstration of masculinity." He tells of Frederic Remington, later a great American artist and sculptor, "dousing his Yale uniform in slaughterhouse blood in preparation for Saturday's game," and of players stamping, gouging, hair pulling, and slugging each other, even jumping on an opponent to break a collarbone in a notorious Harvard-Yale football game in 1894.

College soccer, on the other hand, occupied a peculiar place. Having its roots in foreign lands, the professional game was played by immigrants, and because most immigrants worked in factories, professional teams sprouted from urban, industrial businesses.

Those people didn't care about the college game, which left it to inexperienced players and officials who, "lacking the time and resources [...] found it easier to devise their own rules," Wangerin writes, " [...] in an effort to Americanize the game." That created a stark difference between college soccer and the brand of soccer everyone else was playing and suffocated the developmental relationship that evolved between college and professional football, basketball, and baseball.

Over the decades, professional soccer was nearly wiped out by the Depression and went through an alphabet soup of leagues—the NAFBL, ASL, ASL II, ASL III, NPSL, NASL, MISL, to name a few—almost all with administrators fighting over how to broaden the game's appeal or collapsing under the weight of out-of-control player costs. It just never seemed able to sustain any momentum.

Despite all the complications and confusion, college soccer had its moments. The Intercollegiate Soccer Football Association grew from 36 schools in 1939 to 62 schools a decade later, and 10,000 people attended the 1952 national championship game in San Francisco between Temple and University of San Francisco, which Temple won 2-0. College soccer even played a key role in diplomacy in 1951 when Penn State's team, coached by legendary "Mild Bill" Jeffrey, was chosen to play a series of matches in Iran, of all places—a country that even then was considered very unstable politically. The trip was a huge success diplomatically, even though the Nittany Lions were underwhelming on the pitch.

The number of men's varsity soccer teams continued to grow, totaling about 475 by 1970. By the time I arrived in Bloomington in the early 1980s, that number had grown to around 520, and youth leagues were starting to explode—both of which helped spread the sport. But the unsteady standing of the pro leagues, their disconnection from the college game, and Americans' rabid love of football helped keep soccer a largely overlooked sport on campuses. Remember, the U.S. still was a decade away from what many considered the crucial turning point in modern soccer here: hosting the 1994 World Cup.

The varsity team I cared most about was the one I was clinging to. And, despite my precarious status, I chose to believe that my personal soccer history was on the upswing. At the end of the year, I evaluated and re-evaluated the entire experience and concluded that, while the season had its ups and downs—okay, mostly downs personally—being the 35th man on the roster of a national championship team might be exactly where I wanted to be.

I know it might sound laughable to some, but to me, being the 35th man on a national championship roster was more of an accomplishment than being a starter on a team that wins as many games as it loses. I never thought, *Boy, I could have started at Michigan State and maybe I could have played every minute in the midfield.*

I was part of a national championship team, and I had earned that status the hard way: by sweating and grinding through every practice, every day, week in and week out with absolutely no glory or notoriety of any kind. That realization soothed a lot of bruises to my ego. More importantly, the fantastic end to the season reinforced my desire to stay and push harder toward my dream to somehow, some way get on the field for the cream and crimson. I thought that if this is how it feels to be a redshirt on a national championship team, imagine what it must feel like to be a regular or even a starter. That was about all I needed to get fired up for next year.

For the first time, I started to visualize each and every step of my dream. First, I wanted to make the team, which I'd done. Then, I wanted to dress for home games. After that, I wanted to be on the travel roster, and then start. Finally, by the time I left, I wanted to be a team leader, maybe team captain.

That's the crazy part of life's dreams, isn't it? It's not our plan. It's not our time. It's not when we decide things are going to work. It's placing yourself in a position to succeed, sticking to your goals and objectives, working hard, persevering, believing in yourself, and letting things play out the way they're supposed to play out. Sometimes when we try to control everything, we lose sight of the joy that can come our way on the journey. I certainly did a few times on this journey.

You can look at it in a couple of different ways—it's all about me or it's all about the journey. Sure, I had those definite goals, but I also came to realize that it was almost all about the journey. One stop along the road was being the 35th man.

While I might have become more focused and committed and viewed my status as an ideal start on the path to my dream, the coaches had a decidedly different interpretation, and that scared me.

At the end of each soccer season—fall and spring—three coaches sit down with every player for individual evaluations, almost like a performance review you might get at the office. For some players, it was pretty obvious. Stolly would walk into his meetings and they'd tell him, "Well, Stolly, you led us to a national championship as a starter in the midfield. Your contributions were enormous. We want to thank you for all that you brought to the team this year, and we look forward to you continuing to work hard. Let's set some goals for next season."

For me, the evaluation was going to be different, very different. Who knew how it would unfold? I surely didn't and that uncertainty was a source of extreme anxiety, fear really. Coaches could say anything, but the more I considered the possible scenarios, the more I came up with unpleasant possible outcomes. What in the world were they going to tell me? "Whitey, we thought your positioning of the goals at practice in September and October was perfect." Or, "Hey, Woody, thanks for everything. Good job. Next!"

I felt like I'd worked hard and given it my all to the degree I could in practices. But really, my job as practice meat during the year was nothing more than doing the best—when I got the chance to play—I could to prepare the starters for the upcoming game. Not exactly a critical role, which is one of the reasons the thought of the fall evaluation, my first, scared me. I figured that I had shown enough fight that I wasn't going to be an afterthought. But I had no idea what they were thinking and what to expect.

As it turned out, they were gracious, kind, professional, brief—and brutally honest. They started by saying they liked my character and work ethic. Then they lowered the boom.

"You're never going to play here, Whitey," Coach Yeagley said, and I started having flashbacks to the conversation I had with him the previous summer. I also started getting this sick feeling in the pit of my stomach.

Coach Yeagley went on to say, as he'd said in our talk over the summer in the lobby of Assembly Hall, that IU had a number of starters returning from a two-time national championship team, not to mention another strong crop of freshman recruits. The best high school players in the country were coming to play with the best collegiate players in the country. That didn't leave much room for a guy like me.

"Our goal," Coach Yeagley said, "is to win another national championship, and we feel we've got all the tools we need."

He looked hard at me, wanted to be sure he had my full attention.

"We'd suggest that you transfer to another school, Whitey," Coach Yeagley said, "if in fact you want to continue playing soccer in college."

I was reeling, but I just wasn't ready to give up. I started feeling a little desperate, sitting there in the coaches' office, with them staring across the desk at me, waiting for me to cave. My mind started spinning. *How can I hang in here? What can I do to just keep my hopes alive a little longer? The spring season,* I thought. *The spring season might be it.*

The soccer team had its spring season coming up in about four months. A more informal, seven weeks of games and practices, the annual spring season gave coaches a start on determining the composition of the team for the fall. *If I could just hang on through that,* I thought, *maybe something will break my way. Maybe I'd get a chance to show that I belong.*

"Can I please stay with the team in the spring, and we'll evaluate things then?" I asked.

The coaches looked at each other for a few seconds. Coach Yeagley sighed. Then I thought I saw the slightest smile crease his lips.

"I guess so, Whitey," he finally said.

I felt myself breathe again, thanked them for the opportunity, and got out of there faster than a soccer ball blasted from Stolly's foot. I didn't want Coach Yeagley to have time to change his mind. I remember stepping outside the building and feeling so relieved to have survived.

The problem was that the spring season yielded more of the same for me. I was never considered for the starting team or even the top 18 players practicing on the starters' side of the field. As hard as I played when I had the chance, I made absolutely no impact. In case I didn't get the message during the fall evaluations, the realities of the spring season made it obvious that I was in no one's plans for this team. I had another evaluation, and the conversation was the same as the fall talk.

Again, I asked for another chance—this time to come back for two-a-days in August and practice with the team in preparation for the fall season. The coaches grudgingly agreed, with three stipulations: I wasn't guaranteed a roster spot, I could not stay in the dorms with the team, and, if I wanted to eat with the team in the dorms, I had to pay for that.

In looking back, they probably created those "minor" stipulations as a way to set up an insurmountable hurdle to get me to quit. But at the time, again, my naïveté or my determination or my optimism or my desperation—call it whatever you want—saw the situation in a completely different light. I smiled broadly and sighed.

"I'll take that as a yes," I told them. "See you in August. And, thanks."

Then, like the last time, I shot up from the chair and got the heck out of there before they changed their minds.

It was a close call, but I was still kicking, and for now, that's all that mattered.

Coach Yeagley was a motivator and a true winner.

4

CHAPTER

There were times when I felt all alone
on the practice and game field.

THE LONELY DRIVE FROM COLUMBUS

CHAPTER 4:

THE LONELY DRIVE FROM COLUMBUS

That return wasn't the rousing triumph I would have hoped for, but it wasn't a total failure, either.

The summer between my first and second years, I caught a break when an assistant coach at IU, Mike Freitag, picked me for a team of players from the state to participate in a national tournament. Coaches from each of the Midwestern states would field teams of players from those states and would play to win the Midwestern title. That winning team then would advance and represent the region in a Final Four tournament.

For whatever reason, Coach Freitag liked me, and I, of course, welcomed that. Just to be noticed by a coach who remembered my name, noticed that I was out there working as hard as the rest of the guys, meant an enormous amount to me. He played a key role in keeping my hopes alive. When he selected me to be on the Indiana state team for the summer tournament, I was pretty jacked, partly because about eight of the players were from IU, and being on this team with them helped me determine where I might fit on the Hoosiers' roster next fall. The other reason I was excited was that my brothers Pete and Danny were on the team. For the first time in our lives, all three of us played on the same team.

Except that in my case, playing was a very uncertain prospect. I was on the team but had to assume my designated position on the bench for that weekend tournament in Rockford, Illinois. It was something I expected with such a strong lineup.

But then, early in the first game, Dave Boncek, our starting outside back, hurt his ankle bad enough that he ended up sitting out the entire weekend tournament.

That was my chance. Coach Freitag inserted me at the wing, and I played well, really well. I think those probably were the best three games I've played in my life. I'm sure it had a lot to do with my joy at being on the field with my big brothers and my desire to show that I belonged in IU's lineup that fall. Whatever the reason, I was comfortable and confident and that went a long way toward me feeling for the first time that I could compete with players the caliber of those at IU.

We ended up being eliminated after a tough 1-0 loss to Wisconsin, but that tournament is among the many reasons Coach Freitag occupies a warm place in my heart. He gave me the opportunity to prove what I could do. And, I think he must have planted the bug in Coach Yeagley's ear that I was capable of contributing.

A few days later, IU was presenting a soccer camp at a private school in Indianapolis, Park Tudor. I wasn't one of those selected from the team to participate, of course, but it was just a few minutes from my house so I drove over one day to say hi to a few of the guys. I ended up bumping into Coach Yeagley in the lounge at the end of the day.

"Hey, Whitey," he told me, "I heard you played really well up in Rockford. That's great news."

I was thrilled, of course, that he'd been told, but I just smiled and said, "Yeah, coach, I felt really comfortable. Everything came together pretty well. Wish we would have won the whole thing, but I think the experience helped everybody. And, I really enjoyed being on the field with Danny and Pete."

He smiled and held his eyes on me for a moment, nodding his head. And, I thought something registered. At that instant, I really felt that going into next season, I'd have a chance; that Coach Yeagley at the very least would give me a look, some consideration, even with seven returning starters from a national championship team and perhaps the top recruiting class in the country. Maybe I was going to get a legitimate shot at some playing time, which is all I was hoping for at this point.

But my assessment turned out to be wrong, another in a string of disappointments.

I came to campus for two-a-day practices in August and lived in the apartment. In some ways, I fit in pretty well. Stolly and Keith were my roommates again, and now it sort of felt like I was becoming part of the team. Last year, after practices, I didn't know where I was going to eat, when, or with whom. This year, Keith would say, "Hey, let's go eat with the team in the dorm," and the three of us would walk in together. It was one of those hugely important intangibles.

But, while every other person was treated as a team member— put up in the dorms for free if they didn't have off-campus housing, eating for free in food service hall—I was paying my own way. Like last year, I occupied another version of limbo during those two-a-days. I had no guarantee of making the team.

But, I did survive two-a-days and made the team, and the NCAA allows only one year of red-shirting. So I sort of rose above practice-dummy status. In many other ways, however, my existence was very similar to what I endured the year before.

Now that I was an official member of the team, I was among the 34 guys who would suit up for every home game, although I was pretty much at the very end of the bench. For away games, coaches would allow 18 guys to travel with the team on plane trips; 20 on bus rides.

Most weeks, coaches knew the top 16 or so guys who would be traveling on away games, and they'd open a couple more slots for guys based on how they practiced in the days leading up to the game.

At practices every week before an away game, guys like me—maybe 17 of us—fought with everything we had just for the chance to suit up, if the coaches made an additional slot or two available. Whether we'd play or not after winning a spot was highly uncertain. We just wanted the chance to wear the cream and crimson and ride the bench.

I don't have to tell you that most practices before a road game could get pretty rough on those weeks coaches added a couple roster slots. We scraped and clawed every day in practice for them. And, yeah, some days, fights broke out, or at least scuffles or shoving matches did. The deeper into the season, the more desperate we became, and the harder we worked. And, if you want a great lesson in how to crush a person's drive, try 8 or 10 or 12 weeks of vicious practices without your name being called to suit up. That's what happened to me. I made the travel team once, and that time only because coaches took about 25 guys on the bus.

I remember having really strong weeks of practices and hoping, even knowing, that my name would be called as a traveler only to hear coaches call out two other names. Not only is it depressing, it can tear you apart psychologically.

I deserve to play, and I'll never get my chance, the little voice in your head says. It can get louder and louder. *These coaches don't know what they're doing. They just hate me for no reason at all. I can't believe I'm taking all this crap.*

Once those thoughts take hold in your mind, it's a short trip to Quitsville and clearing out your locker. Guys did quit that year, every year, because they couldn't deal with the constant disappointment and physical toll. I don't blame them. It's humiliating, and physically and psychologically exhausting, especially after a high school career that probably included over-the-top accolades. Leaving may have been the only way for them to preserve their sanity and self-esteem. I certainly considered leaving at the time.

But I also remember somehow sensing that the guys who were losing their drive were going to sap my motivation, too. It became something of a subconscious survival mechanism, I think. I drifted away from them and toward the optimistic guys, the guys who were playing.

See, I sort of lived in two worlds that would overlap a little: the informal world of the apartment with my buddies Stolly and Keith, and the formal, intense world on the field and in the locker room.

When the three of us would hang out in the apartment, they'd give me a shot in the arm from time to time about something I did in practice and talk with me about areas where I could improve. After grinding out my red-shirt year and sharing the national championship run with Stolly and Keith, they'd fully embraced me as a teammate by my second year.

Our friendship grew and strengthened to the point where Stolly and Keith would invite me along with them wherever they went. One of those places was practice. They'd always leave early and stay late and always ask if I wanted a ride. I always said yes.

I'm sure that when I'd step on the practice field, some of the upperclassmen studs looked at me wondering what the heck I was doing there early, acting like I belonged when I didn't. But I tried to ignore the stares. After a while, they simply got used to seeing me around. I was no concern to them. As long as I stayed out of their way, they probably figured what difference was it that I was there. I'll tell you the difference: I learned another component of how champions are made—through extra hard work, what I call the habits of champions. I became accepted even more, and somewhat subconsciously, as part of the team. I also think that after a while, the upperclassmen probably respected the fact that this guy who never had a chance of playing was working to get better, to somehow, just maybe get on the field. The truth is I did get better by practicing that extra time every day. Of course I would, but the gratification was nowhere near instant. In fact, I might call it distant gratification.

The other advantage I had living with Stolly and Keith is the exposure I got to all the upperclassmen players who would stop by the apartment just to shoot the breeze. It was an incredible learning experience to be around great players, in addition to Stolly and Keith—guys like Paul DiBernardo, Pat McGauley, Mickey McCartney, Dave Boncek, Mike Hylla, and others.

They would talk about practice, talk about what's needed to reach a championship. After a while, they even started mentioning stronger aspects of my play and my personality that boosted my confidence about being on the right track. I would try to absorb and apply everything. I'm sure I absorbed some lessons without even knowing it. And, being a sophomore gave me a little more credibility and courage to speak up. My freshman year, I'd sit back and listen almost always. By now, they'd seen me around enough to accept me as part of the team. I could contribute to the discussion every once in a while, and they'd acknowledge it as part of the flow. I was being woven into the fabric of the program and learning so much about what it takes to be a successful soccer player at IU—lessons I could carry to many parts of my adult life.

I also was fortunate in that I was well-liked by the guys. Maybe it was something I developed from moving around so much as a kid, but I found that as much as change generated a lot of anxiety, even fear, in me as a kid, I could adapt pretty well to new situations. I think they saw early on that I wasn't some goofball. I followed team rules, worked hard at practice, tried to stay upbeat and bring a certain camaraderie and fun wherever I could. I like to think that was one of those small things that—together with other small things—had a cumulative effect. I was building toward something, although I'm sure I was fairly clueless that was happening.

So, yeah, the two worlds of the apartment and the practice field would overlap. But, mostly in that formal, intense world of practice and locker room, Stolly and Keith and the rest of the guys had their hands full trying to play at the highest level, keeping the team on track toward a third consecutive national championship, and managing all that came with those responsibilities. They didn't have time to bother with me, to worry about how I was playing, whether I was progressing, how I was doing emotionally. They were all business.

That's where Coach Freitag helped. At practices and in the locker room, every once in a while he would come up to me and check in. Many times, it was nothing more than a simple, "Hey Whitey, how you doing?" Other times, he'd say he liked what I was doing. He'd tell me to hang in there, that I was going to get a shot, that I was going to make an impact. He never made a big scene about it, but he made a point of doing it, and I was really grateful then and now.

And my parents, for all that I was making them endure, were incredibly supportive; although looking back, our relationship at that point served as a pretty enlightening, delicate, even funny example of the parent-child dynamic.

I wasn't secretive with them about my feelings and thoughts during the whole odyssey, but I wasn't totally transparent, either. I guess you'd say I was semi-transparent; I exercised selective recollection with my mom and dad.

I don't remember complaining about my soccer tribulations, and my parents say I never did. At the time, I felt like I'd burdened them enough already. I simply didn't want my mom and dad to worry about how their son with the crazy dream was doing down in Bloomington. I knew if I told my mom I didn't sleep last night because coach said this or that, then she wouldn't sleep for three days, or maybe she'd make the hour and a half drive down to try and make me feel better. I needed to grind it out. I knew what I signed up for, and I was going to work through it.

So, I would tell them, for example, "I didn't have a good practice today but tomorrow I'm going back out there." I'd try to share something positive. "Stolly actually said I played a nice ball out of the back that one time," I'd say.

Knowing my parents as well as I did, I figured they could sense if I was in really deep water emotionally, that I would have reached out to them in some fashion, and I would have. But I was growing up, and I think I felt it was time for me to be a man about this. After all, it was my decision and I needed to experience the valuable lesson of meeting challenges. I know now that if struggles and mistakes are avoided, or we're guarded or blocked from dealing with them and the consequences, the smallest of speed bumps will cripple us.

It came down to this: My parents were there for me, which was the best scenario. I never would have survived if I didn't have their unconditional love and support. No one survives without love and support from somebody. Simply having them on the other end of the phone line, genuinely listening to me and keeping me focused on getting through the next couple of days, was an enormous blessing. They'd tell me to concentrate on the things I could control and try to keep me upbeat. They attempted to give me the tools to deal with my issues on my own, which was exactly what I needed. After those phone calls, I always—always—felt better, like somehow, no matter what, things would be just fine. I had received enough good energy to carry on for the next day.

What I found out later, and what makes me laugh—and get a little choked up— today is that, of course, my parents were agonizing privately over my rocky journey. They were going crazy wondering how I was handling all the rejection and failure. They were talking a lot about how much or how little they should get involved, dissecting every little scrap of what I told them. They struggled with allowing me to grow through these challenges or coming to my rescue. And, they didn't want to agitate or worry me unnecessarily; just like I didn't want to worry them. Parenthood. It's a funny, beautiful thing, eh?

I did have this much going for me: As one of the 34 or 35 guys who dressed for home games and rode the bench, I actually did get on the field a couple times, but only in the last three minutes when we were leading 5 or 7 or 9 to nothing. It's called garbage time, and I was a garbage man. Or mop-up minutes, and I was carrying the mop.

Talk about another emotional downer. I almost dreaded it when we'd be shellacking some poor team and the clock would tick down to the final couple minutes. Coach Yeagley would scan players on the bench, call out the names of everybody on it with a sweep of his arm and unload all of them onto the field, like prisoners spilling from the back of a truck. I and probably the three or four other guys who were scrubs would sort of seize up anticipating his gaze.

When my name was called, I'd cringe inside, but pop off the bench, pull off my warm-ups and start jogging in place, stretching, getting ready for my 90 seconds of glory. It was humiliating for me to run on the field. People in the stands, if any were left and if they noticed at all, would shout out a sort of laughing cheer that sounded more like a jeer.

But, a funny thing inevitably would happen. After a few seconds on the pitch, my love for the game took over. My mind seemed to let go of all the embarrassment, and all I saw was me playing soccer for Indiana University, the best darn college team in the country. And, you know what emotion swept over me? Appreciation. That's right. Call me stupid, naïve, ignorant, whatever you want. But, even with all that was churning inside me, I appreciated having the chance to take the field.

It was during that time when I struck another milestone: I played and sweated enough in one game to actually need a shower. It was at Northwestern, the one bus trip I made that year. By halftime, we were up 4 or 5 to nothing. Coach Yeagley inserted me at wingback, which at IU is a really cool position that requires speed, agility, endurance, mental toughness, and focus. In other words, it requires talent. You're getting up and down the field, involved in just about every aspect of the game. It was THE position I wanted to play at Indiana.

I stayed at wingback the entire second half, and while no one mistook me for a superstar, I played solid, mistake-free soccer. After the epic, perhaps happiest shower in my two years at IU, I sat in the locker room, feeling like I may have taken another tiny step toward my goal, when several guys came up to me—Dave Boncek, Mike Hylla, Stolly, and Keith. Each of them said how well I'd played and encouraged me to keep working hard. That was a moment that helped me believe that I belonged. The five-hour bus ride back to campus was long. I was tired, a little sore and boy, did I feel great, like I was floating, instead of rolling down the highway.

The only problem was that moment came in September, early in the season, and nothing more materialized from it. No momentum. After the Northwestern game, I never traveled with the team. Then came the Ohio State game and maybe the most dispiriting experience of the season.

A few weeks after the Northwestern game, we were traveling to Columbus, Ohio, to take on Ohio State. Or, I should say the rest of the team was traveling. I wasn't in anybody's travel plans. But Coach Yeagley tossed out an option to those like me, who weren't among the 18 or so guys traveling on the team bus. If anybody wants to drive up to Columbus on his own and can arrive at the stadium on time, Coach Yeagley said one day at practice, those players would be allowed to dress, sit on the bench and have a shot at playing.

It was nearly a four-hour drive. I probably could get my hands on a car, but like many college students, I was short on cash. I and most guys viewed the offer as no offer at all, as another chance to be embarrassed. I'd worked very hard again that week, had very strong practices, and thought I deserved to be invited, not extended some half-baked invitation. I was angry. My feeling, and those of the rest of the mutts in my predicament was, *Hey, if I'm part of the team, the least you could do is put me on the bus and haul me to Columbus and back.*

Not Stolly, who had a tendency to keep things simple, to see things in very stark terms.

"Whitey," he told me after practice, "you have got to demonstrate your commitment and your interest in this. Honestly, the coaches, this program, they don't need a guy like you."

I was silent. He was right and I knew it, but still…

"It's up to you," Stolly said. "You don't have to go and you don't have to be part of anything, or you can suck up your pride and take them up on the offer they extended, which is what I would do if I was you."

"I don't know," I told him, and I went through my litany of reasons: no cash, the hassle of getting a car, the long drive there and back, my anger at constantly being overlooked and dismissed.

"If I had aspirations to be part of this team, I would drive over, sit on the bench, and be part of the team," he said. "Simple as that."

"I won't play. You know that, right?"

"Maybe," Stolly said, "but one thing's for sure: You won't know until you try, and you're definitely not going to play if you're back here sitting on your butt."

I thought, *Yeah, easy for you to say.*

"And, you know what?" he said, "Even if you are right and you don't play, I still think you should do this. You've got to demonstrate your interest in being a part of this program. Don't let them off the hook by boycotting something. They give you a chance to come, come. You should take advantage of any shot to be part of the team, be around the starters, be around the coaches. They see a guy drive all that way, they know he's committed to the team. They know how badly he wants this."

That was the quintessential Stolly. If coaches ask you to go lift weights, go lift weights. If they ask you to move goals or fetch soccer balls, move, fetch. If they call you because a recruit's coming in, go meet the recruit. If they ask for a cup of coffee, you ask if they want cream and sugar. You don't want to give the coaches any reason to think that you're not 110 percent committed to the program.

Stolly can be a very persuasive guy.

After thinking about it for a couple of days—mostly under his relentless pressure to make the trip—I borrowed a car, scraped together gas money, packed a few sandwiches and drinks, and followed the team bus like some sort of weird groupie. I was the only guy who drove, but I'd made up my mind that this was a great idea and I was pretty excited. While we rolled down the highway, I'd wave to the guys and laugh. We were all having a great time. No awkwardness whatsoever.

When we arrived, I grabbed my gear from the managers and dressed in the locker room. Then I found a place to squeeze in at the end of the bench and was ready to play.

Let's just say that it was a great seat to view the action. I didn't play one minute in a close game that IU won. Coaches didn't say three words to me. After the game, I walked back to the locker room, changed, and got in my car.

Sitting in the parking lot, I felt like a real clown, an ignoramus. I was so embarrassed that I waited for everybody to board the bus, watched it leave, and stayed put for another hour, staring out the windshield at nothing. I figured that was better than making a bigger fool out of myself by riding alongside the bus, letting the guys see me the whole way back to Bloomington and think about how big a goof I was.

That drive was one very lonely, mostly dark, long stretch of I-70 for me, one in which I did a great deal of reflecting on just what it was I was doing and on how much I was willing to humiliate myself for a dream that seemed to be moving farther from reality.

I could have blamed Stolly. I could have blamed the coaches. I could have heaped hatred on myself. During those 230 or so miles, I probably did a little or a lot of all those things and more, in my head and out loud. *What was this dream about anyway? Was I trying to satisfy a warped, out-of-control ego? Did I think I was heading for professional soccer? Was I trying to get girls? Did I have any self-esteem whatsoever?* I'm glad traffic was light. If the interstate was crowded, any motorist passing me would have been deeply concerned and probably called the state police alerting them to the kid in the car talking to himself.

I'd like to tell you that I finished the drive and worked through all those issues with a really clear understanding of why I was still trying to play soccer at this national powerhouse. But, I didn't, not really. The drive did give me enough time to immerse completely in self-pity and then slowly pull out of it. In the end, I told myself, it was up to me how to interpret all this, how I wanted to handle it. It wasn't Stolly's fault or the coaches' fault. It wasn't even my fault. I made the decision with eyes open and this particular day didn't break my way. So be it.

I tried to focus on what Stolly had said. The coaches and the rest of the team saw me at the game, on the bench, and there's no substitute for showing a commitment better than by getting your ass up early and standing right there in front of someone saying *I'm ready. It's a long shot but I'm willing to take it because that's how badly I want this.*

I decided by the time I pulled into the dark parking lot of our apartment that maybe it was the right thing to do—to show them that I viewed myself as part of the team, regardless of how they viewed me. Being on the bench at a road game was significant, I told myself. Maybe it placed me one tiny step closer to achieving the dream, planted a seed in the coaches' consciousness about my commitment that maybe they didn't even recognize at the time.

I guess that trip was a little like faith itself. You're really not sure what's in store or why exactly things happen, but you go ahead and take a chance, act on your instinct. You trust. The short-term looks pretty bleak, but long-term? Well, maybe the Big Guy Upstairs has more important plans for you long-term, and He's seeing if you've got it in you to follow through, or He's grooming you to be ready for those bigger plans. He's always teaching us; I know that much. Back then, I know I didn't comprehend all that, but I'd made peace with the decision, put it behind me, and was ready to continue the chase.

I got back to the apartment well after the team had arrived on campus and dispersed. I trudged up the steps, pushed through the door, and there he was, studying at the kitchen table: Stolly. Keith had gone to the library to study, but Stolly knew I'd be looking for him, and he wanted to be there for me. That was the kind of guy he was. That was how tight we were.

When I saw him, I have to admit all the hurt rushed over and through me, nearly two years of it. I broke down, sobbing. He got up and gave me a hug, cuffed me on the back. We sat down.

"Whitey," he said in a soft voice, "you still did the right thing. I'm telling you, it was the right thing. I'm surprised you didn't get in. I'd hoped that you would have gotten to play, but you didn't, and nothing's going to change that."

He let me continue crying, which I did. He let me vent and gripe and moan, to say how frustrated I was. He even allowed me to say how I thought Coach Yeagley was screwing me over.

And, that's when he spoke up, when he said something I thought was pretty cold.

"I respect the coaches' decision."

At that point, I thought I could have used a little sympathy and commiseration, and I felt the sting of his words. But Stolly was imparting another really valuable life lesson.

One thing he would never do and would never agree with me about was trashing the coaches. I think he viewed that path as a way for a guy to direct responsibility someplace other than on his shoulders, a crutch for a player, an excuse. And, I think he knew that bitching about a coach being unfair would lead a player to pout, work less, and that would lead to a lower place on the roster and that would lead to... well, you get the picture. It's a ticket to that place I talked about earlier, a place I didn't want to go: Quitsville.

Stolly knew I didn't want to quit, and he didn't want me to quit. He believed in me and wanted to push me to stay as tough mentally and physically as I could, to get even tougher. At the time, I might have been hurt by what he said. But looking back, I see the importance of that moment, among the many I spent with my friend Stolly. Later I would see just how badly he wanted me to play for IU. He would do more than talk about it, much more.

* * *

The one bright spot during all this darkness wore crutches and got out of a car across the street from my apartment complex one cloudy fall afternoon. I would later discover that her name was Sherri Seger. But, at the time, all I knew as I watched her hobble across the street and into the apartment complex was that I was drawn to her.

She had that certain something beyond physical beauty that I couldn't quite articulate. A style, a grace, a warmth. It was unmistakable, and I sensed all of that before I'd even met her simply from seeing her that first time trying to navigate her way over the pavement.

I had an urge to run down the steps and help her across the street—the whole carry-your-books thing—but I was pretty intimidated by her. She was just so beautiful. I simply watched for a few seconds until she disappeared from view.

It turned out that she lived in the same apartment complex a few buildings from mine. The unit she shared with her roommates was right beneath the one where my buddy and teammate Mickey McCartney lived. Mickey and I had become close my first year, when both of us were red-shirts but on completely different trajectories. He came to IU from St. Louis as an All-American high school player the year before I arrived. As a freshman, Mickey played quite a bit. Then he suffered a nasty ankle injury and was red-shirted his second year to give him extra time to rehab. He was a really social guy, and, just my luck, Mickey and his roommates got to know Sherri and her roommates. I found out, after learning her name, that she was a remarkable athlete—a state champion high school gymnast on a full scholarship at Indiana—and was incredibly fit, even though she was injured.

I wouldn't speak to her for weeks, couldn't stir up the nerve, really. But I kept my eye on her and that electric smile. I knew a chance existed, if I timed things right, that I might be able to force a "coincidental" meeting at some point in the future. So, I bided my time and looked for an opening that wouldn't appear too obvious, but just obvious enough, if I could ratchet up my courage.

What was funny about the situation was that as much as I wanted to get to know Sherri, I never felt that I had even the slightest chance of dating her. Something about her beauty, her poise, her class made it seem that she was out of my league. My soccer exploits were the same. I didn't have a chance in hell of being a serious player on the team. The coaches all but scratched my name off the roster every chance they got.

And yet, I took a completely different approach to soccer. I would do anything to play at IU and would never give up until they escorted me off campus. With Sherri, it was a full-fledged secret crush. The only person I told was Mickey, who kept it confidential. I told him everything because I liked and trusted him so much. I was content to be patient and allow the romance never to materialize if it wasn't meant to be. I never did in fact force the issue and never came on real strong, just kind of kept that warm feeling in my heart and that little butterfly in my stomach every time I saw Sherri. Mickey would ask me about her every once in a while; he'd ask, among other things, if I ever was going to ask her out. But for the most part, he respected my shyness toward her and knew that it probably never would happen.

Though I believed I never had a chance of dating her, I admired Sherri a lot and wanted to get to know her. I guess in the end I just felt it would be great to count her among my friends. I'd be happy with that. Really. So, I decided I might be spending a little extra time at my pal Mickey's apartment, in part to see who might happen to be around.

Except that I really didn't see her around the apartment complex for a long time. In fact, the first time I did see her—after she emerged from her car on crutches—was in the training room at Assembly Hall, IU's main athletic center. She'd destroyed her ankle in a gymnastics meet the winter before and had to undergo surgery to repair it. But that surgery didn't work completely, so she had to endure a second one. I'd seen her hobbling across the street shortly after that second procedure. A few weeks later, I saw her in the training room, which I happened to be walking through on my way to the locker room one afternoon before practice. She was near the windows, stretching and going through some therapy on her ankle.

I was startled to see her, and I'm not sure I was able to contain that spark. But, I figured this was a great time to make my Big Move.

"Hi," I said, smiling, beaming maybe, probably blushing, too.

"Hi," she said back and flashed the Sherri smile. Dazzling.

And, I kept right on walking, not knowing what else to say.

Okay, so I didn't exactly sweep her off her feet with that one. But now I knew how I'd be able to see her regularly. She'd be in the training room every afternoon working on her ankle. As luck would have it, soccer practice started around the same time as her rehab session. I wasn't hurt, but I just happened to make my way into the training room—hey, a guy needs some ice once in a while, some tape, too, needs to check in with the trainer to see if he's got any important information about the latest advances and technologies to pass along—almost every day to get a glance and go out of my way to make eye contact or say hello or stare. It wasn't exactly stalking, but I looked forward to those encounters, even though I never felt it would ever be anything more than that.

Time went on and our encounters became more frequent. As one of Mickey's buddies, I was tossed in a group of about 10 that included all of his and Sherri's roommates and assorted peripheral friends. The entire group, or parts of it, would hang out a lot, whether it was having lunch or dinner, studying, walking to class, or simply sitting around shooting the breeze. And, although the various combinations never really put Sherri and me alone together, I did get to know her. We became friends, and I was glad to discover that she really was exactly who I thought she was from my very first impression—a gentle, kind, happy woman with a big, electric smile that she displayed often. The better friends we became, the more I liked her. Still, I never let anyone except Mickey know how much I truly liked her.

On the soccer field, my exploits continued to be pretty futile. I worked my ass off in practice but rarely got playing time in games. I wavered about staying with the team but just wasn't ready to quit. I might have figured I still had two more years and anything could happen. Or, it might have been the strong season the team was having.

That year's version of the soccer Hoosiers was one of the best I'd seen. It was made up of an unbelievably rugged, smart, team-oriented collection of extremely talented players who worked very hard and studied the game. The leaders, including Stolly and Keith, led by example, arriving at practice 30-45 minutes early to work on individual skills. Then, after an hour and a half of team practice, they'd stay and work more. They all had a commitment to be great, independent of any pushing from coaches. I'll never forget that.

Before witnessing that level of commitment, I had thought a team could rest on its laurels, that they could put it on autopilot. When you're that strong, I figured you can just show up, concentrate, and win.

These guys taught me it's the extra work that always makes the difference; you have to put in that focused, additional effort to reach a performance level above everyone else and to make that level your norm. Even though I wouldn't fully appreciate it for a while, being around that team was something that served me well beyond my soccer years. It taught me how to prepare physically and mentally for all sorts of challenges; how to focus; how to be a teammate who could motivate and help your teammates be the best they could be without nagging or making them hate you; how to set and accomplish team goals and the combination of elements it takes to be a champion.

And, the guys loved playing soccer, playing IU soccer. They had their eyes, minds, bodies, and souls fully focused on winning a national championship. Anything less would be a disappointment. I may not have fully appreciated it, but I was nearly awestruck watching it unfold.

We started the season by beating San Diego State 2-1 and then reeled off seven consecutive wins—many really close, which showed how important mental toughness and extra preparation was—before playing a 1-1 tie with St. Louis University. We followed that with another 10-game winning streak, and by the time the regular season ended, we'd won 19 games, lost 1, and tied one. We were primed for the post-season tournament.

My game was improving steadily, too, even though I barely played during the regular season, and I was very focused on making the tournament roster.

In my mind, I felt like I'd done the things to earn that spot, without ever having to look at it from the coaches' perspective (which I didn't). They might not have noticed anything. But I was telling myself, *Gosh, I'm working hard. I'm playing well.* I wasn't scoring 50 goals but, in my mind, I'd shown such improvement. *What else do I need to do? I thought. I'm doing everything they're asking of me and more. I deserve this.*

Getting on the tournament roster worked the same way as getting on the regular season travel roster, with an encouraging tweak. A couple of spots were available that everybody had to fight like piranhas for, but the coaches also were going to keep a few extras to practice during the NCAA playoff run. Those extras wouldn't suit up, but at least they would be part of the team by practicing every day with the group and getting to enjoy the excitement of the post-season.

I was realistic. I knew I had no chance whatsoever of making those two final roster slots, dressing for games, and playing in the tournament. But I did feel I had a legitimate shot at being on the practice squad, and I'd be ecstatic with that.

But again coaches saw it differently. When they called out the names of all those who'd stay with the team, mine was never mentioned, and that was tough, really tough. It not only hurt to think I'd worked so hard and made contributions that merited a slot on the lowly practice squad; it fueled my personal doubts. *Was I really good enough to play here? Was I delusional and a complete fool for continuing?* It took a few days to shift out of self-destructive mode, but I did, partly because of all the excitement of the post-season tournament.

I like to refer to that run as bittersweet cool. As bittersweet as it was, I still got caught up in the tourney electricity, and it was really cool to watch my buddies, particularly Stolly and Keith, drive toward a championship.

We started the playoffs by clobbering rival University of Evansville 5-0 then exacting revenge on St. Louis, beating the Billikens by a 4-2 score. Several of the tourney games were at IU, and I watched them from the stands, thrilled to see the guys make their run.

It was at that time that Keith and I started a little ritual. On the morning of games, we'd go to church and then sit in empty Bill Armstrong Stadium for about a half hour. It was almost like a download session in our little sports sanctuary. In the quiet, we'd envision how the place would look, how the game would unfold, how it would feel. And then we'd go to the pre-game meal.

It worked. In the tournament semi-final we beat a tough Hartwick team 2-1. Indiana had returned to the championship game for the third straight year. One team stood between the Hoosiers and three consecutive national championships: Clemson.

The finals were in Seattle and televised live by ESPN. I couldn't make it out there this time. Just too expensive. So, my family hosted a big party at our home in Carmel to watch the game, which was particularly weird for me. I didn't know what to feel. Yeah, I was part of the team. Heck, I had toiled away since August with the guys, played in a few games, and yet here I was, in my jeans and cream and crimson IU t-shirt watching the game on TV with a group of fans. I felt this bizarre, strong disconnect. *I'm part of the team but not really part of the team.* And, particularly after one conversation at the party, I heard that little demon in my head asking whether I was doing the right thing by hanging in there at IU. It made me think of that definition of insanity: doing the same thing over and over and expecting different results.

I'll remember that championship game for a number of reasons, but one that sticks out is the playing surface. Kingdome crews had to convert the surface to a soccer field from a football field, and that changeover made the turf very slippery. IU didn't have the proper cleats for it, and we were slipping all over the place. In the end, it may have been the difference, maybe not. We'll never really know, but Clemson scored first. We tied it and the game stayed that way for a long time. Then Clemson scored late and beat us 2-1. It was a staggering loss, one that would haunt us years later. The house party ended in deathly silence.

That championship game was Keith's last, and it's important to note that, at the time, he was one of two IU players in the history of the program to go to Final Fours in each of his years on the team. Pretty incredible. That says a lot about the caliber of teams we had and Keith's leadership skills.

It was one thing to watch the loss on TV, but when I rushed back to campus that night to meet the guys at the apartment, Stolly and Keith understandably were in deep depression. I remember hugging them and not saying a word. After a couple of years living and playing together, we'd become as close as brothers. I knew there was nothing I could say to ease the pain and frustration.

They mentioned something about the wet playing surface but really didn't talk much at all. Our apartment was like a morgue, and it would stay that way. I remember all of us having a really tough time just getting out of bed and going to class. For about a week, it felt like they and I were completely shut down. No rocking chair talks. No long walks on campus. No practices. Season's over. Nothing to do. Semester's coming to a close. All of us just sort of stayed out of each other's way for that week or so, trying to let everything pass.

Stolly and Keith and all the guys worked so unbelievably hard and had played so well. It was a shame and yet the season still was a remarkable one. How many teams and players would trade places with our guys that year? Every single team and player in the country except for the guys from Clemson. Those are the things you completely lose sight of when you get so close to winning a national championship.

One saving grace in those dismal winter days was that I knew when we'd return in January, Stolly would be there. My man Stolly. He had another year before graduation, and that gave me a little spark to carry on. But I still had to make it through evaluations.

Every evaluation during my career scared the sweat out of me. Every single one of them. I knew they never were going to be filled with praise. Far from it. Those sessions with Coach Yeagley and a couple assistants—the walls surrounding us with framed certificates of dozens of All-Americans who played at IU—always felt as if I were nearly begging or madly scrambling to offer them a reason to let me hang on.

But I figured this year my chances of moving way up were pretty strong. I'd gotten a little playing time, at least in the regular season, and I'd kept a really upbeat, team-healthy attitude throughout what anybody would consider a miserable existence. We also were losing seven starters, which meant the deck was going to be reshuffled; replacements had to emerge. Who knew at this point how everything would settle?

About a week after the Clemson game when I walked in Coach Yeagley's office for my evaluation, I could tell the coaches were still recovering from the loss. I think they viewed my session in particular as a pain in the neck, or as if I were a little gnat buzzing around that needed to be addressed.

It was short and not very sweet. Coach Yeagley told me they had no idea where I fit in this team, but that they'd learn a lot after spring soccer, and I didn't like the way he said it. Didn't sound reassuring. In fact, his tone of voice made me very nervous.

Then it was over. Nothing about me working hard to earn playing time last season. Nothing about showing my commitment by driving to Columbus. Nothing much at all. I got up, thanked them, walked out, and felt pretty empty. The entire meeting lasted about four minutes. Pretty eerie.

A few days later, Keith graduated. We didn't have one of those dramatic goodbyes. No tears. That just wasn't Keith's style. Besides, anybody who has been a college student knows that the days leading to winter break sort of dissolve in the frenzy of studying for and taking finals so students can get the heck out of town for a busy holiday homecoming. That's kind of what happened with the three of us. The campus started shutting down for winter break—maybe that was a therapeutic thing for the soccer team—and Stolly, Keith, and I scattered.

Keith went on to play professionally in Kansas City, married his longtime girlfriend from Kansas City, and raised a family. Today, he lives in the St. Louis area and works as a regional manager for a telecommunications company where he's worked for more than 20 years. We're still friends, of course, and get together whenever possible. One other thing: His son Tommy fell in love with soccer, too. Guess where he played his college ball some 20 years later? Yep. IU. And, the number on his jersey? 20, same as his father wore.

* * *

I ended up playing well that spring when I got my limited chances, which fueled my enthusiasm for the upcoming season. But that enthusiasm was snuffed at evaluations. Once again, my view of the situation was wrong, very wrong.

"Whitey," a blunt Coach Yeagley told me during my evaluation in his office, "you're never going to play here. We like your work ethic and your attitude and the players really like having you around, on the field and in the locker room. But, we've got a very strong recruiting class coming in this fall, best this program has ever had."

That recruiting class was more than very strong. It was considered by many to be that year's strongest batch of freshmen soccer players in the country. We were simply reloading a team that had won two consecutive national championships and played in a third. A guy like me who thinks he's moving up was sorely mistaken. The freshmen arriving in the fall already played better than I did. They were gunning for the starting lineup and would have a very legitimate shot. Let's face it, the coaches are going to give their star recruits, guys they've been fawning over and pursuing for months, a lot longer look than some mutt walk-on who barely made the team. So, I was in a no-man's land, and the older and more experience I got didn't necessarily improve my chances, not if IU was going to continue to bring in the best recruits in the country. It was almost as if time were squeezing me out, working against me.

I swallowed and felt my heart pound. Coach Yeagley took a moment then looked me right in the eye.

"Look, Whitey," he said, "I need to be honest. You just don't have the talent to play at this level, and I don't think you ever will. Have you thought about transferring, maybe to a smaller school? I think it'd be a great move. You'd probably have a terrific experience someplace else; some less competitive program."

I didn't say anything for a couple seconds. Then I scrambled to find a few words about looking forward to August and seeing how things would go. He didn't look encouraged. The session ended in awkward silence.

Pushing through the doors of Assembly Hall, I was overwhelmed with hurt and fear for my future. All the work that I thought was moving me up in the pecking order. All my fragile optimism. Crushed. I was reeling, angry again and filled with self-doubt.

One thing was clear after that: It was time for me to go elsewhere, or at least look at alternatives. The opportunity actually had presented itself in that conversation I mentioned earlier, while watching the NCAA championship game at that party in my parents' house back in December.

I had talked quite a bit with former high school teammate Ken Veilands at the party. After graduation, Ken went to University of Southern Indiana in Evansville, where he was the goalkeeper. The USI Screaming Eagles were a very competitive Division II team. Division II, by the way, is an NCAA classification for intermediate-level sports programs, primarily at smaller public universities with more modest athletic budgets than big-time schools. Placing those schools in Division II gives them a lower profile but a realistic chance of having success in a pool of universities and colleges with similar financial commitments to sports.

Ken was working on me, singing the praises of soccer at his favorite Division II school, USI.

"You know, Whitey," he said, while we watched the game, "you could play there right now."

He reminded me that another of our high school teammates also was playing at USI; that it was a great school; that we'd have a blast playing down there—again—right away.

I stood there thinking about my less-than-encouraging prospects at IU and considered Ken's enthusiasm. Maybe the heartbreak of losing the final game was at work, but I figured it was time to be realistic about all this. By the end of the party, I told Ken to go ahead and mention my name to Coach Mike Ferrell. He must have taken me at my word.

A few days after the final spring game, right around the time of my highly un-inspiring evaluation, Coach Ferrell called me. We met for lunch at the Country Kitchen in Carmel. I decided not to tell Stolly. Stolly being Stolly, he might have a tough time understanding. I felt like I needed to think this through on my own.

Over burgers, I told Coach Ferrell I couldn't make any promises, that I didn't want to mislead him, but I was considering a move. I was looking around a little.

"That's great, Whitey," he said. "Smart. You want to consider all your options and make the decision that's best for you."

He gave me a pretty powerful sales pitch on USI, telling me all the things that Ken had mentioned, and I was all ears. Playing with a couple of high school buddies, and especially playing right away, sounded fun. The drive to Evansville would be a little longer than to Bloomington but it still was very manageable. He talked about the difference between sitting on the bench throughout a college career and being on the field all the time. He said I'd make a strong impact on a team that already was pretty competitive, and that sounded exciting, like we could go on a deep run in the post-season.

"We'd love to have you, Whitey," Coach Ferrell said. "Let's get you down to campus so you can take a look around and see what you think. You won't be disappointed."

By the time we were finished with lunch, becoming a Screaming Eagle sounded pretty cool and sensible. I told him I'd think about it and get back to him.

And I did think about it, for exactly one restless night.

I woke up the next morning and knew I was staying at IU. It was the same as the time a couple summers earlier when I went out with my buddies after the cold reality chat with Coach Yeagley and thought Michigan State was the place for me. Until the next morning. Then, the exact opposite was the right thing to do.

That's another curious element about this entire journey. The dream just would never go away. It almost made me angry sometimes. I don't want to get too overdramatic here, but it now feels a little like what happened was destiny. Even with all the rejection and humiliation I had to endure at IU and all the temptations of other places—I'm sure I could have called Coach Baum at Michigan State and he would have taken me back; he'd told me as much — I couldn't shake this dream to play at IU. I knew this much: I didn't want to play at an average place. I wanted to push myself to the very limit and then some to play for the best team in the nation. I wanted to play at the highest level with the greatest group of guys I could or kill myself trying.

Why? That's the tough question, especially considering the kind of player I was. People ask me all the time: How could I be so stubborn, almost foolishly pig- headed? I can't explain it. Something wasn't allowing me to leave IU soccer. Maybe, at the time I'd met with Coach Ferrell, I wasn't satisfied I'd exhausted all my chances at Indiana; that a shred of hope still existed. Throughout the journey, I would contemplate my scenario pretty regularly, usually sleeping on it then going with my gut, which told me to hang in there and keep pushing. I've pretty much always been a go-with-your-gut kind of guy.

I got back to Coach Ferrell the day after our lunch and to his credit, he understood about pursuing dreams. He was a total gentleman.

So, I closed that door and turned again toward IU, where the only beam of light from my spring performance was barely a sliver. I'd played just well enough to get invited to the two-a-day practices in August without having to pay or try out for a slot. Everything else was up in the air.

It was a very precarious existence and not at all where I'd expected to be entering my third year. But as the summer approached, a reason for renewed hope emerged: I called it The Stolly Iniative.

5

CHAPTER

*I never thought that the thrill of walking
without a limp could be so rewarding.*

RE-LEARNING TO WALK

CHAPTER 5:

RE-LEARNING TO WALK

Being from Virginia and going to school in Bloomington, Stolly didn't get home often. So, I'd invite him back to our family's place every once in a while. My parents loved him, which meant, in part, they'd stuff him with all the Greek home cooking he could handle.

As close as we'd become, the one thing that really bothered Stolly and me was that we'd never played together during an IU game. We talked about it, dreamed a little about how great it would be—how much fun we'd have and the electricity we'd bring to the team. But I wasn't holding up my end of the bargain.

"Whitey," Stolly would say while we'd knock the ball around, "you gotta get tougher. You've got great skills. Your one-touch ability is dynamite. You run the field well. You know the game as well as anybody, and you're a great team player. All the intangibles, man. But you're the nicest guy in the world. And, that just doesn't work out there. You need to be tougher mentally and physically."

He was right, of course. I was trying, but I just really didn't know how to get from where I was to where Stolly felt I needed to be.

Stolly knew, and he felt so strongly about our friendship and our dream of playing together on the field that he made a huge commitment to me one afternoon right before we left for the summer.

"Tell you what, Whitey," Stolly said, "I'm going to stay back in Bloomington this summer, go to summer school, and you and I are going to train together."

I didn't know what to say.

"Stolly…" I stammered.

"I'm going to teach you the toughness you need and, come fall, you'll be ready, readier than you've ever been. When the season starts, you and me are going to be on that field together, Whitey. Me at center mid; you at left mid. And, we're gonna kick some ass."

It was an unbelievable offer. If Stolly was known for one thing, it was toughness. He was one of the most rugged, tenacious players in the nation—qualities that would serve him well when his soccer career took off a couple years later. For him essentially to volunteer to be my personal trainer thrilled me, to say the least. Knowing he believed in me that much and was willing to offer so much help gave me such confidence. And, one thing about me was that I was always ready to work. My thinking was the more work, the merrier the worker, especially with Stolly. Any lessons he was willing to impart I was willing to work at and absorb.

So that's what we did. When his class schedule was open for a few days, he'd drive up to our family's house and stay with us, which he loved, of course. Every time he'd arrive, my parents treated him like a prodigal son. They pretty much treat every visitor like a prodigal son or daughter. On the days he had class, I'd drive down to Bloomington and stay at our apartment for our training sessions.

We worked pretty much every single day on fields in the hot, humid summer of central and south central Indiana, often three times a day. We'd run distances and sprints over and over, of course. But, the most difficult part—and the part that improved my game the most— was our one-on-one drills.

Toughest was the 50-50 balls. For those unfamiliar with soccer, a 50-50 drill is when two players stand directly across from each other about five yards apart with the ball between them. They count to three then dash for the ball and fight to gain control. The player who succeeds and pulls away from the other wins. In the game of soccer, it's pretty well known that you've got to win the individual battles all over the field, and that's what Stolly was trying to beat into me with this little exercise in abuse. His biggest emphasis was to get me to really want to win that ball, not just feel satisfied by getting in the tackle and pressuring the opponent. He wanted me to have a very defined purpose with every 50-50 ball and go for it with everything I had.

Simple, right? Yep. And, very grueling, especially if you do it time after time after time against one of the toughest players in the country. Going after a 50-50 ball with Stolly was like going against a brick wall with the legs of a linebacker. I had no way to finesse through it. The guy was so strong and so gifted at using his body that most of our matchups early on would have been laughable if they weren't so painful. What I discovered was that I was either going to get tough or break my legs. So I tried to get tough, and he didn't back down.

We also had a one-touch drill, which actually was a lot of fun but also exhausting. We'd stand 10 yards apart from each other and play the ball back and forth, each of us allowed only a single touch. The objective was to kick the ball to a place—feet, shins, hips, chest, head—where the other guy could play it back with one touch. If I hit a ball 20 yards over Stolly's head, for example, I'd get a point. If he kicked a ball too far behind me, he'd get a point. First one to 10 points loses. We played this one in particular for hours and hours, and it was brilliant in its simple, high intensity. Mentally, one touch was demanding because you had to stay focused. Physically, it was even tougher because you're on your feet—mostly on your toes—moving like crazy. In essence, you had two guys competing in a routine designed to break down the opponent while you were wearing down mentally and physically from the opponent's pressure. And Stolly, as you might guess, could rip a ball. He'd routinely send it at my shins at 50-60 miles an hour. Punishing doesn't begin to describe it.

Finally, we had the head drill. My heading needed a lot of work. So, Stolly would stand 30, 40, and 50 yards from me and launch balls in the air. I'd have to run them down and try to head the ball all the way back to him. When players head a ball, they typically do one of two things: let it hit them in the head or attack the ball. I had a tendency to let it hit me in the head. Stolly's head drills were designed to get me to attack the ball without fear, and it took a while for me to get it. Sometimes, I felt like I'd gone 10 rounds with Muhammad Ali.

Throughout every drill, Stolly made it clear that he wasn't there to make me feel good about myself by slacking off. He was there to make me work harder by beating me time and time again, every day, and telling me specifically what I needed to do with each drill. This was an exercise in tough love. Stolly knew only one way: tenacious. His pursuit of life always registered at about 140 percent, and this summer training program was the ideal platform for him to show it. He was pushing me past my breaking point, making me understand that the only way he was going to make me feel good about myself was if I outworked him.

Progress was slower than I'd hoped. In late July, I came down to Bloomington and moved into the apartment for the upcoming semester, which was about a month away. That was the real push, three weeks of intense training that nearly broke me in two. We'd walk over to the soccer practice field by Armstrong Stadium, warm up, run, then go at each other.

After a few days, I started noticing that I was using my body better. I'd gotten stronger, going after a ball as hard as Stolly would. We'd shove, and instead of me getting knocked on my butt, it was him a time or two; sometimes both of us would fall. I could tell he was proud of me for pushing him around, not giving an inch, darting in and out, and I was winning my share of 50-50s.

My one-touches started to be more precise more often, too. By early August, I could last as long as he could most days, and my headers were stronger and more accurate. Every once in a while, I even sensed Stolly's aggravation with my physical play, which made me grin a little, although I wouldn't let him see.

As my skills, strength, and stamina grew that summer, so did something just as important: my confidence. By mid-August, I'd elevated my play two or three levels. I was a machine. I was so ready, so well-oiled, so physically and mentally prepared to play at IU that fall that nothing was going to stop me.

I could never thank Stolly enough. He didn't need to be doing what he was doing. The guy was a star, but he had such a generous heart to take me on as a project. At the same time, I give a lot of credit to myself. I never backed down from his challenges. Sometimes, he'd spontaneously call and say, "We're meeting at 2 o'clock. Let's go." I would always be there and always go as long as he wanted. I could have backed out of those three-a-days any time and, although Stolly would have been disappointed and aggravated, it certainly wouldn't have had a lasting effect on him. But I didn't. I stuck my nose in there every day, got smacked around, and happily kept coming.

I think he found that particularly fulfilling. Any time you mentor somebody, if the level of commitment isn't reciprocal, the relationship is headed for a dead end. It's one thing to have someone take you under their wing. It's another to want to do it, to want to work as hard as I wanted to work. In my case, I reciprocated big time. Stolly never let his foot off the gas, and I never let him. We complemented each other in that regard and both came away from the experience feeling great.

Those few weeks taught me another important lesson. Hard work—really hard, focused work—is a skill, just like agility or speed or jumping ability or hand-eye and foot-eye coordination. It's a little different in that hard work is a skill you develop. Too often, I think, we place all this emphasis on "natural talent," or smarts. Don't get me wrong. Those can play a part. But the more I go through life, the more I appreciate that choosing the right attitude—and it is a choice—getting back up after being knocked down, staying motivated to work, and being resourceful are what matter in life's successes and failures. If you've got those, chances are strong that you'll get where you want to go. And, even if you don't make your preset destination, the ride will be a wonderful one, and the place you end up well worth the trip.

All that effort from Stolly and me coalesced at the perfect time. He and I and a few others reported to pre-season practices a few days early, a tradition for IU soccer upperclassmen. I was in the best physical and mental condition of my life. After two years, I knew the coaches and system well enough, knew what I needed to do in pre-season to catch their attention, which was one of the reasons I'd reported early to pre-season workouts. I was going to build momentum for my great season.

Coach Yeagley wasn't overstating the situation when he'd told me we had a strong crop of freshman. Three of our top five recruits were the top three players in the country. They included John Johnson, the best player in the soccer hotbed of St. Louis; Dave Gauvain, John's strong high school teammate; Pete Stoyanovich, player of the year in Michigan; Herb Haller, player of the year in Ohio; and Sean Shapert, the all-time leading goal scorer in Pennsylvania high school soccer history. All five—John, Dave, Pete, Herb and Sean—were *Parade* magazine All-Americans. In addition to those guys, Coach Yeagley once again had tapped the international market, bringing in a highly touted Dutch kid, Han Roest.

Those guys were expected to come in and fill most of the spots made available by the seniors who'd left, and the team would stay right at the level it'd been the previous year. The objective at IU is for the quality never to drop an inch from one season to the next. Every year, the goal is the same: win a national championship, and coaches felt that these freshmen, with help from a few upperclassmen, were up to the task.

What did that scenario mean for me? The Big Squeeze. Even though I'd been around two years, I had no advantage whatsoever going into my third year, not even close. I was a non-scholarship guy, which meant the coaches had no investment in me, which meant they had absolutely no incentive to play me. Of those seven spots vacated by guys who'd graduated, exactly none had my name penciled in. I not only had to overcome the players who were returning—guys like Stolly, Tim Hylla, Rod Castro, and other reserves—I also had to out-play these heavily-recruited, highly-touted freshmen.

But I knew that months earlier, which was why I'd prepared, why I'd worked through The Stolly Iniative. I was ready, a little nervous, yeah, but confident and mostly just excited for what was ahead.

One emotion I lacked was anger. It's funny in a way, I guess, but anger was never a motivation for me. I was never angry to prove the coaches or those players who doubted me were fools, or to show that the freshmen—whatever the year—weren't any good. I never thought, *I'm going to rub their noses in it, show them that they all were wrong.* In fact, I was the opposite. I liked and respected the coaches immensely. Why else would I have come to IU and stayed? I'd also gotten to know a lot of top-flight recruits already and liked almost all of them. They'd typically stay with Stolly and me for their campus visits, mainly because Stolly was a superstar, nationally known, and pretty much the face of the program for his time at IU. As his roommate, I was the benefactor of bonding with these guys, building camaraderie from the start. To this day, JJ (a.k.a. John Johnson) is one of my very closest friends, and our relationship began on his recruiting trip. We hit it off right away, and there's no denying that he'd earned his All-American stature. I didn't want to shut him down, defeat him, rub his face in it. He would become my teammate and close friend. I felt much the same about Stoyanovich and Shapert and Herbie—all terrific guys who could and would help the program on and off the field.

Was it a little strange entertaining guys I knew were coming in to push me back farther down—if that was possible—the roster? Yeah, a little. Did we compete against each other later once they committed? Absolutely. But we believed that competition was healthy, that it is the essence of sport, and that the deserving player would win time on the field. I wasn't going to be angry about that. My job as a host on their recruiting weekends was to get them to fall in love with IU and sign a letter of intent as quickly as possible so that we could have them and remain a preeminent program. I embraced that responsibility gladly. Whatever happened as a result would happen. If it meant that I was sitting on the bench, so be it.

By the time other upperclassmen arrived that August, Stolly and I were pretty settled in the apartment. On late afternoons into the early evenings, the 12 or so of us who'd gotten to campus early would scrimmage on the practice field next to Armstrong Stadium. It was informal, without coaches, but very intense. Any time you step on the field at IU, whether it's a scrimmage or just a kick-around, it's never easy. These aren't for Sunday afternoon picnic or rec league players. The mentality of an IU soccer player was and is to be the best every time you take the field. This particular year, with all the vacant positions left by guys who'd graduated, upperclassmen were asserting themselves, trying to stake their claims to those positions as early as possible. So, when we'd do these little 6-on-6 games, everybody was all business.

That first night, I got after it right away; I jumped in the fray and played well, better than I'd ever played in practices. I was faster, stronger, and had that edge Stolly wanted. Guys noticed. I could feel it in the way they approached me on the field that night and for the few days after.

The night before our last informal practice, Stolly and I got back to the apartment, and he made the meal he was most proud of: chicken, rice, and pierogi. I have to admit, for a guy who didn't cook that often, it was a mouthwatering dish. He wanted to celebrate our effort over the summer and the promise of us finally taking the field together for the cream and crimson. We sat down and dug in.

"Whitey," Stolly said, "you're going to be something special this year. You're going to play, and you're going to make a difference. We're going to play together, and we're going to be tough, really tough."

Stolly didn't BS people. He said those words with such conviction, I nearly got goose bumps. Two years of hanging in there and giving more than I ever imagined had set me up to succeed, to achieve my dream. He was fired up about it almost as much as I was.

I started visualizing that first morning of coach-supervised, two-a-day practices. They begin with a morning run of two miles that everyone must complete in 12 minutes, a pretty challenging physical and mental test. This year, I couldn't wait for it. Stolly and I had been running like madmen for weeks, and I had my sights set on finishing first to give coaches something to think about right away: that Whitey belonged with the best players at IU, and that I was setting pretty high expectations for the entire team.

During the last night of scrimmages, I must have showed my enthusiasm because Timmy Hylla came up to me and said how much I'd improved.

"You keep this up, Whitey, you're going to be on the field in no time," Timmy said. "It's amazing how good you've gotten. Keep it up."

Two things made his observation stand out. First, Timmy was in the same class as me, but he came in as a highly-recruited freshman, cracked the starting lineup almost immediately, and played in the national championship game. He then followed that up by being a starter his entire sophomore season. In other words, he was a major contributor to the program while I was hanging on by my fingernails.

Second, he was truly happy for me. I felt the same vibe from all my teammates for much of my time at Indiana, but especially during those scrimmages. Yeah, they were surprised, but pleasantly, and they were excited for me. That kind of energy was like a lightning bolt to my motivation and confidence. I was ready to jump over the bleachers at Armstrong Stadium to play.

Not 10 minutes later, the final scrimmage was winding down, and I was feeling great. The Stolly Initiative meant I had no fatigue, no pain. It was hot and thick with humidity—this was, after all, south central Indiana in August—but I loved it. I approached the ball, planted my right foot, took a shot with my left, and felt something snap in that foot I'd planted. Didn't think anything of it, really. I'd heard plenty of snaps and pops from my body over the years. I played for another 15 minutes or so, limping around and feeling the pain hanging on, toward the outside of my foot, and I was trying to assess how badly my right foot was hurt. It felt like if I could just crack it, sort of like cracking a knuckle on a finger, it would feel fine. The problem was I couldn't crack it, and the pain refused to subside. *It couldn't be broken,* I thought. *Maybe it's a strain of some sort. I'll play through it. Ice it tonight.* But after those 15 minutes, I couldn't go anymore. And, I just remember thinking, *This isn't good.*

Practice broke up. Stolly and I got some ice from the training room, and he hauled me back to the apartment, where I placed the bag on my foot for about an hour. The pain wouldn't go away. I tried to step on it a couple times and felt this throbbing along the outside of my foot.

"Stolly," I told him, "I think this is more than what I thought it was."

No trainers were on duty so he suggested we go to the hospital, where a doctor examined me then ordered an X-ray. An hour or so later, he came back to my curtained vestibule and said it looked like a strain.

"No big deal, really," he said. "You've got to stay off your feet for a few days. Keep it iced and elevated. We'll get you in a little protective footwear, some crutches, and you'll be fine in about a week."

I was bummed. Given my status on the team, just three or four days of lost time at the start of this particular season would be a setback, lost time that I might not ever be able to make up. We had those phenomenal freshmen, and I knew how important it was for me to make a strong impression the first day of practice—especially running those two miles—and in the crucial early days of two-a-day practices. That's when coaches gauge who the starters will be and how the 18-man roster will take shape. If you're a returning All-American or one of the prized freshmen and you've got a sore hamstring or something, it's no big deal. For an unproven guy like me, every minute of those practices that I miss really hurts. I knew that by the time I got back, I was going to have a whale of a time playing catch-up. I hobbled out of the hospital about midnight, aggravated, trying to figure out how I could get back as soon as possible.

But the next morning the throbbing was worse. Stolly told me I should see our athletic trainer Johnny Schrader. I can't remember if I got an X-ray or what, but I do remember that Johnny told me a few seconds after examining my foot that it was more than a strain.

"This is a little bigger deal, Whitey," he said, and I could tell he was trying to gently broach some very discouraging news. "I think it's a broken bone, and what I'm really concerned about is that it might be the fifth metatarsal."

"What's a metatarsal?" I asked.

He explained that the fifth metatarsal is a long bone that extends behind the baby toe. It can fracture for any number of reasons—

simple stress, or a stretching or pulling of the tendon that attaches there can yank a piece of the bone free.

"One of those breaks is something called a Jones Fracture, a break at one of the slowest healing bones in the body," Johnny said.

I started feeling sick in my stomach.

"If it's a Jones Fracture," he added, "it gets complicated."

"How complicated?"

He sighed and explained that it's one of the slowest healing bones in the body because blood circulation to that spot is very minimal, and you need blood circulation to help bones heal. Even after someone recovers from a Jones Fracture, named for the British doctor who researched and wrote about the injury, it often reoccurs.

"It definitely would be season-ending and could require surgery," Johnny said. "Could also end your soccer playing career. It all depends on the healing."

Career ending? I thought. A shock fired from my stomach to my brain. I felt a headache coming on. I asked what would happen for me to need surgery.

"If it doesn't heal properly, they'd have to go in and insert a screw."

He must have seen my face, which I'm sure registered shock.

"Tell you what: let's not think about that right now," Johnny said. "Let's just hope it's not a Jones. Come on back tomorrow morning after the swelling goes down a little and things look a little clearer."

Now, I was really scared, but I tried to think positive. I told myself it was probably a bone bruise or something, anything but a Jones Fracture. It had to be. A lot of ice, alternated with heat, keeping it elevated, and I'd be back on the pitch in a few days.

The next morning, I thought that maybe, possibly, the pain had eased a little, but when I put weight on it, I felt that pain deeper than the day before. Stolly took me to the appointment, even went to the trainer's room to meet Johnny, and was I ever glad he did.

I could tell by Johnny's expression that the news was grim.

"It's a Jones Fracture, Whitey," he said. "I'm sorry. Really I am. But we gotta get you in a non-weight-bearing cast right away. You're going to have to stay off it for a minimum of 10, maybe 12 weeks. Then we'll see what the bone looks like."

It wasn't a total surprise and yet my body reacted like it was. I honestly couldn't believe what Johnny said. Just didn't register. Then, it felt like a trap door had been pulled from under me, and I was falling into a black, empty space without landing. Stolly was silent. I'm sure he couldn't believe it either. He knew I was done for the season, and he'd worked and invested so much in my dream. It was part of his dream, too. All of it evaporated in front of his eyes.

In about 36 hours, I went from being poised to seize the dream I'd worked so hard for—playing for the best college soccer team in the nation—to being shut down for the entire season. For a guy like me, losing an entire season was tantamount to disappearing altogether. I had to work my ass off to get this far. After three months, coaches wouldn't even remember my name. Then, there was the part about possibly needing surgery, about the chances that a fracture would end my career.

I had no emotion for this. It was so staggering. I just sort of stared at Johnny, who was very sympathetic.

"I'm sorry, Whitey," he said again. "Like I said, let's not get too far ahead of ourselves. Let's take a look at it again after 10-12 weeks and see what we've got; see how well it's healing."

"What happens if it's not healing at that point?" I asked.

He waited a couple seconds, sighed.

"Well, we've got options. We could hold out a few weeks longer—"

"And then what," I interrupted. "I mean, if it isn't healed after we wait that extra time?"

Johnny stared at me a moment.

"Surgery," he said softly. "If it doesn't heal after we wait, we'd probably have to perform surgery then see how the bone had mended, but..."

Johnny's voice trailed off. I knew what he was leaving out. After surgery, the chances of me playing again would be very, very slim.

He put me in a cast right there. I kept the crutches. Stolly took me back to the apartment, and we barely spoke. What was there to say? He had to get to practice. I had to wallow. I knew he was sad, too, and I knew he had to start thinking about moving on without me. That's the nature of team sports. Somebody drops out, but the games must be played. A program like IU's didn't shut down when All-Americans were felled by injury. When a guy like me drops out? The coaches wouldn't even shrug. I was way at the back in the storage room of spare parts. They had a team of superstars to assemble.

Back at the apartment alone, I sat staring at space for a while, and then I broke down. Just couldn't believe the bad luck I'd had. How unfair this was. I know, I know. I brought it all on myself. Like I'd told myself dozens of times before, I made this choice. Somehow, that didn't ease the frustration that day.

I went in to a deep, self-pitying mode, and it lasted for days. All I kept thinking about was how hard I'd worked, how much I'd improved, and how ready I was to achieve the dream. Now, I was done for the year. Plus, I had no wiggle room on my years of eligibility. The NCAA gives you one red-shirt year, and I'd used up mine as a freshman.. From a soccer standpoint this year was a waste, burned to ashes with nothing to show for everything I'd accomplished through all that hard work.

On top of all that I heaped the sad realization that Stolly and I would never play together, which was almost as heartbreaking. We'd started as chance roommates and became brothers, really, who were so thrilled and inspired by the idea of taking the field together that we'd worked for more than three months to make it happen. Now it never would.

I told myself to snap out of it, to calm down, that I was going to come back. But then I thought about what Johnny had said, that surgery was a distinct possibility, that this is a career-ending injury for some players, and I would sink farther and farther.

It was the lowest I'd ever been, and I didn't see a way out. What I wanted was pity. I wanted people to tell me how sorry they felt for me. I wanted attention. I had no focus on the bigger picture of how the team was going to do. It was all about Whitey. *Why was this happening to me? Why now? Why couldn't I catch a break?* The anger, again, wasn't present. But whining self-pity was.

One thing for sure: I was ready to quit this asinine dream. I was done. But, even if I quit, I thought, what school would take me? At best, I was damaged goods. At worst, my soccer playing days were over. Besides, I'd fallen in love with IU — the school, the people, the atmosphere, the community. Soccer or not, I doubted I could leave the place. Was I destined to limp around campus as one of those pathetic guys who couldn't stop feeling sorry for themselves? Who bored other people with stories about what could have been?

I did get that pity I so selfishly wanted. My parents were sympathetic. Stolly and other guys on the team genuinely were bummed for me, too. But people can do that for only so long. They, like everybody, had their own issues, daily concerns, and challenges that needed attention. At that time, I was an energy vortex, an abyss that sucked enthusiasm from everyone around me. How much could I expect them to endure? Besides, time rolls on and you start to feel pretty sick of yourself in that mode. I actually did start to get a little angry for once — at myself. *What a baby,* I began thinking. *Stop whining and crying and get on with your life.*

Which is what I think was at the foundation of what happened next. I didn't give up. While I sat there at my lowest point on the journey, feeling sorry for myself and my right foot, something happened. I've thought a lot about it and, just like all the other times I'd decided to hang in there when things looked bleak, it's difficult to articulate. Being sick of my woe-is-me attitude definitely had something to do with it. Maybe stubbornness, too, or the embarrassment of facing all the doubters. The idea of losing an identity that was so wrapped up in that team also played a part. Or maybe it was just that—again—I hadn't felt I'd actually gone the full distance; that if I somehow could come back, I still had a shot. I guess I started thinking that unless somebody forced the end on me—unless the coaches locked me out of the practice field—I wasn't going to do it to myself. If a glimmer of hope existed, I was going to let that little light of mine shine, fan the weak flame, and feed it until it glowed or all the fuel was gone. And, the more I thought about it, the more I believed I had the fuel, which in the end, I guess was my love of the game at this place at this time, my love of a challenge and my love of a journey, no matter how treacherous and arduous it can get.

Maybe this has become obvious at this point, but something else played a big role. At my core, I am an optimistic person. I just can't stay down for too long. I'm one of those people who got lucky or is truly blessed being raised in a family who believes that hope can never be extinguished until the breath of life passes from us. We almost radiate hope. Sometimes I think our entire family tree sprouted from the optimism seed. All of us, including my grandparents, are or were people who believe that life is rich; that we have much to be grateful for every single day. We believe that you can come through setbacks and by doing so, become better, wiser, more empathetic, and fuller. Coming through those can, yes, make you even more hopeful that the human spirit perseveres.

For a combination of those reasons, I came to the conclusion that I could be miserable or I could be part of the team. I could fall back or try my best to move forward. I gave it more thought for a couple days, and in a strange way, the idea of staying and working through this ordeal and taking ownership of it became empowering, liberating. I tossed my inner whiner to the shoulder and let the persistent optimist take over driving. He was more fun to be around anyway.

I started thinking about where I was and how to get where I wanted to go. I was very expendable, nearly invisible to the program, and I couldn't let that continue. I couldn't become an even tinier figure on the horizon over Coach Yeagley's shoulder. Priority number one, I decided at that point, was to stay connected to the team.

So, I returned to practice and was determined to stay in shape, which lead me to concoct what I admit was a rather strange regimen.

I'd arrive at practice on time, hop on the stationary workout bike in the training room and ride it, pumping my one good leg while resting my casted right foot on a chair, for an hour. Then I'd go up to the cinder track around the soccer field at Armstrong Stadium—a track where the Little 500, made famous by the blockbuster 1979 movie *Breaking Away*—is run. While the team practiced next to the stadium, I'd jog—more like hobble-jump—on my crutches for two miles around the track. Eight laps. The first few days, all I could manage was a walk. But I learned how to handle my light-weight, metallic helpers so that soon I gained speed and ran, or at least moved very quickly without letting my right foot touch the ground or falling flat on my face. It turned out to be great aerobic exercise and my armpits eventually toughened up. It also must have been highly entertaining for my teammates, who would sneak glances at me.

After those two stations, I'd work on my left-foot ball skills and finish the day by attending the team's strategy sessions. Then, every night back at the apartment, I'd string a couple of wires from an electric stimulus device to a node on my cast near the top of my foot. I'd flip a switch on the contraption and let it run for a few minutes, which the medical staff told me would stimulate blood flow in that area and help the bone heal better.

Every few days, I'd go to the doctor for a check-up, hoping that the news would be great; that I was getting the cast off in a day or two. Didn't happen. The doctor kept telling me I just wasn't ready yet. Two more weeks, he'd say, and I'd sigh, let myself drift into self-pity mode for a few seconds then slap myself and get after it again.

The psychological aspect was maybe tougher than the physical tedium of my rehabilitation. I kept battling the negativity and lethargy that crept into my mind. Those were telling me to disappear completely, to miss my rehab assignments and pick it up later when the cast came off. Some days I would get after my curious workout regimen a little less enthusiastically than others. Those days it seemed that these setbacks were just another part of my journey's overlying theme: This wasn't meant to be. It's just not going to happen. I'd still drag my rear end through the daily routine, though, and every time after I did, I felt a little better, like I was taking charge, doing everything I could to come back, that I was moving forward, even if it was baby steps.

Life is full of lessons if you choose to look at it that way. And, you know what? I learned something pretty crucial during my one-legged odyssey: If you really want your dream bad enough, you can't care how you look going after it. Many people must have thought I was nuts riding the bike one-legged, hobble-jogging around the cinder track. I'm sure I looked insane. And, early on, I sure did feel, well, uncomfortable. But I'd made up my mind. I was all in. I was a member of the IU men's soccer team, and I was coming back. I wanted this so bad that it didn't matter what people said or thought. I would tell myself that I wasn't absorbing their negative vibe or doubt. I chose to be oblivious to it. I was headed in the totally opposite direction—forward on my stationary bike and hobbling on the oval on my crutches. I still had a chance, I'd tell myself, long as I was walking.

During that time, I never missed a practice. I did, in fact, remain in a non-weight-bearing cast and on crutches for 10 weeks, finally getting the cast removed in mid-October. I was really jacked, thinking I could jump right back into action. Then I got a look at my leg.

Compared to my rock hard left leg, the right one, especially below the knee, was so withered it looked a little like a thick, hairy spaghetti noodle. And it was weak. Very weak. Apart from the muscle atrophy, the bones in my foot, ankle, and leg were frail from lack of use. The whole appendage from my knee down had atrophied so much I could barely stand on it. I thought of what Johnny Schrader had said about the possibility that the bone hadn't healed well, and I worried how in the world the fifth metatarsal inside this limp appendage could possibly be healthy.

I wouldn't know for weeks. At that moment, much of my future depended on the second stage of rehab, the post-cast stage, one I'd given almost no thought to. Johnny set benchmarks for me, starting from a pretty basic concept: I had to learn to walk again and hope that the bone would strengthen thoroughly while I increased my stress on the right leg.

I had to wear a shoe on that foot at all times except when I went to bed at night. My first stage was walking on concrete or similar hard, flat surface. When I stopped limping on that surface, I could walk on grass. When I stopped limping on grass, I could jog on pavement, and when I could jog cleanly on pavement, I could jog on grass. If I could do that without limping, I was ready to wear cleats. But then I had to start all over walking on grass in the cleats, then jogging in them. Each of these little markers took a week or two, a very tedious and frustrating time that seemed to stretch into forever.

I remember days when I couldn't wait for 3:30 p.m., when I'd stand in front of Johnny and try to prove to him that I wasn't limping.

"Ready?" I'd say.

"Ready," Johnny would say, his expression a mix of amusement and skepticism.

I'd walk for about 20 feet, turn and repeat.

"You're limping, Whitey," Johnny would say.

"I'm not," I'd say, and I'd walk it again.

"You're still limping, Whitey," Johnny would say.

I'd exhale, swear to him that I wasn't.

"Yes, you are," he'd say.

"No I'm not."

You get the picture. Multiply that little scene about seven times, and you'll have an idea of what our exchanges were like on a regular basis. Johnny won the debate every time. I wanted to push through each step early, and he was calm, firm, and deliberate—and absolutely correct, by the way. But it shocked me how long it took to regain a natural gait, and I kept worrying whether that little fella, the fifth metatarsal, would hold up.

Throughout this time, I also went to every game, serving as something of a bench jockey cheerleader. By doing that, I was getting to know all the new guys and keeping my friendships going with the others. I enjoyed that immensely. Instead of focusing on my injury, which kept me on the outside looking in, I made a conscious decision to be grateful just to remain a part of the team. Was it hard? Awkward? At times, yeah. I think I could have contributed on the field that year, and it would have been so cool playing with my boy Stolly. I even might have started a couple games. But that wasn't going to happen. No sense in dwelling on it. I needed to make the best with what I had.

It turned out, however, that the team probably could have used the help.

We started that season by losing four of our first five games and then rallied through the middle part of the schedule to earn 10 wins before collapsing at the end, losing three of our last four games. We finished the regular season with 11 wins and 8 loses, mediocre by IU standards, especially after last year's team completed the regular season with 19 wins, 1 loss, and 2 ties, then ended the NCAA tourney with an overall 22-2-2 record.

Our team chemistry was a little sour. As captain, Stolly's high-intensity, demanding leadership style butted heads with some of the other upperclassmen and was more than many of the newcomers could handle. As strong as those newcomers were, they were still freshmen. Some didn't pan out as expected. Others were struggling to make huge adjustments to compete at a top collegiate level, something I certainly could relate to.

We did manage to make the post-season tournament, barely, and won our first game 3-0 over the University of Akron in Bloomington. Our next opponent was University of Evansville at their place—always a tough venue and a tough team. They had beaten us 3-0 earlier in the season.

My rehab continued to slog along, but I kept pushing, and two days before the Evansville game, Johnny cleared me to practice. The bone that was so tentative, that threatened my soccer existence, had met its challenge. I was so proud of the little champ I would have kissed him if I could have stretched to reach my foot. I felt pretty much the same about Johnny, but settled for a handshake, manhug, and about seven heartfelt, rapid variations of "Thank you so much, Johnny. Thank you so much."

I walked in the locker room and never before relished with so much emotion the simple acts of sliding on my shin guards and socks, pulling on my grubby practice gear and cleats. My blessed cleats. It felt indescribable to be there, doing this, hearing the clicking of the cleats as I walked across the concrete and asphalt to the practice field for the first time in three months. I'd missed the entire season and, of course, wasn't even an afterthought to make the tournament roster. But I could practice. I was here, back. It was a glory-hallelujah-thank-you-Jesus moment.

In a telling indication of what was happening to our team psyche that season, I got to the practice field and barely anybody said a thing. I could sense we were gassed and a little agitated with each other.

Johnny permitted me to participate in only one drill, called the 5 v 2. Every day, we'd warm up by having five guys form the outside of a loose circle while two positioned themselves in the center for a game of keep away. The five guys on the outside would keep the ball from the two in the middle. If one of the outside players would lose the ball to a guy in the middle, that outside player went to the middle and was replaced by the guy in the middle who'd snagged the ball. It's a great, little warm-up drill that starts to sharpen some basic skills.

Never before did I carry so much love—I mean love—for a 5 v 2 drill. I think I smiled for the entire 15 minutes. Then Johnny forced me to sit out the rest of practice. I stayed anyway, watching. Walking back to the locker room, I told a couple guys, "Hey, win this game so that I can get another practice in next week." They looked at me a little strangely, but chuckled. That's all I wanted: to keep the season alive so that we could keep practicing so that I could stay a part of this.

Didn't happen. We went down to Evansville and lost 3-0 again. Season over. My third year amounted to 15 minutes of practice. At the latest in my perpetually-anxious evaluations, coaches again gave me little reason for hope. They had no idea where I fit.

"You know, Whitey," Coach Yeagley told me, "we just don't know what to tell you. You had an unfortunate injury. We haven't seen you practice the entire year. We're really not any farther along with you. So, it's awful difficult for us to give you any type of evaluation."

Can't say that I was shocked by that, and I really couldn't disagree with him. Hey, at least he remembered my name. At least I wasn't cut, and believe me, that thought entered my mind.

"Let's see what happens in the spring," Coach said, "and we'll make a determination then."

For the next few hours, all I could think about was that I was three years into this program and didn't know where I was. Neither did the coaches. *I'm almost back to square one,* I thought, *back to being a freshman who barely made the team.*

Thank God I still had enough positive energy flowing from the comeback to fuel my determination for a strong spring season. And, I did have a decent, but not great, spring. The time off hurt me and my evaluation was pretty much the same as the one a few months earlier. I thought I had a shot at making the 18-man travel roster, but I'd thought that before and been disappointed time and time again. August loomed, and I could feel anxiety stirring again.

After the spring season, Stolly hung around, training with the team and with me. In the spring of 1986 he was drafted by the Cleveland Force professional indoor team, and my family hosted a huge send-off party for him. He played in Cleveland for a couple years and for the U.S. national team during that time, including the 1987 Pan American Games in Indianapolis. He followed that by playing for the U.S. in the 1988 Olympics in Seoul and the 1990 World Cup in Italy. Every time he'd return to the U.S, within a week he was at my folks' house, weighted down with flags, souvenirs, and other memorabilia that he'd lavish on us while he shared stories of his adventures. We loved those moments probably more than he did. It felt almost like a son and brother was coming home after serving abroad in the military or in the Peace Corps. Such wonderful memories.

We did end up playing together a few years later in a couple of amateur tournaments in Indianapolis, and it was fun. But it made me a little mournful about what could have been.

Today, Stolly's married with two kids, working in the financial industry. He lives about a mile from me, and our relationship is as strong as ever. He even talked me out of retirement when we were in our late 40s to play on an indoor soccer team with him and a bunch of IU soccer alums, which turned out to be a fateful decision. My first pass to him was wide. When he tried to play it, he tumbled and broke his leg.

Didn't matter. The game throws its ups and downs at us, but Stolly and me, we endure. That's how it is with brothers.

John Stollmeyer was a 4-year starter at IU and went on to represent the US National team in the World Cup.

CHAPTER

6

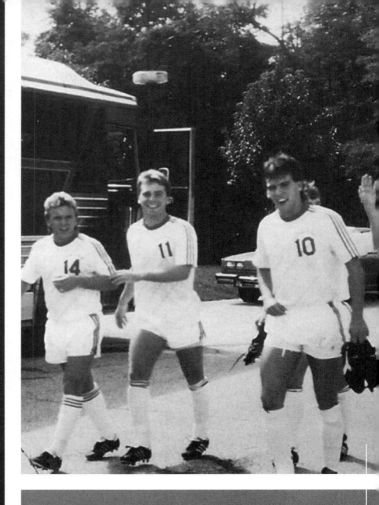

Walking up the hill for my first-ever career start.
Flanked by JJ (#11) and Stoyo (#10) with Kenny
Godat, I was ready to go.

THE RUINS OF REDEMPTION

CHAPTER 6:

THE RUINS OF REDEMPTION

Of all the big-time athletes who passed through IU—Isiah Thomas, Mark Spitz, Antwaan Randle El, and Lou Saban, to name a few— one of the bigger deals was Pete Stoyanovich. A three-sport high school athlete out of Dearborn, Michigan, Pete chose Indiana because he wanted to play football and soccer. The Hoosiers football coach at the time, Bill Mallory, and Coach Yeagley agreed to let him kick for the football team and play forward for the soccer team.

As pro football fans know, Pete went on to become one of the NFL's most accurate and consistent place kickers in a 12-year career with the Miami Dolphins, Kansas City Chiefs, and St. Louis Rams.

But before all that, he came to Bloomington as a high school senior for a recruiting visit. Although he didn't stay with Stolly and me, I met Pete and liked him right away, as I'm sure many people did. Picture a young Tom Cruise, an outgoing, super charismatic guy with an enormous amount of talent and drive. Pete and I barely spoke on that visit, but I saw him again a few months later at a soccer tournament, after he'd committed to IU, and told him how much I was looking forward to having him join the team. He acknowledged that he was pretty excited, too, and we chatted for a couple minutes. That was about it.

That upcoming year, Pete's first, was my lost season in a lot of ways, except that he and I started a friendship that would overcome—and oddly enough, strengthen because of—devastating, unimaginable loss.

One of the barriers to our friendship was his schedule, which was more than frantic, especially for a college freshman. His daily routine was to practice with the football team for a couple hours, then hop on a golf cart and zip over to the soccer field to practice with us for about two hours. His weekends were a blur of airplane and bus rides. He'd regularly play for the football team on Saturday afternoon, then catch a red-eye plane flight or bus ride to meet the soccer team—usually in the wee hours of Sunday morning—and play for us that afternoon. Then, it would be back to his dorm room and a return to the weekday grind of classes, practice, and studies.

Pete's was such a rare existence that *Sports Illustrated* stopped on campus for a feature about him. "Often, when I get back to my room on a Sunday night," he told the magazine in 1985, "I think, 'What am I doing?' My weekends go by just like that. I don't understand why I'm doing this, but as time goes by I'm getting more and more used to it. And, it's a good feeling to know I can handle it."

By the next season, Pete had adapted much better. Things were also looking at least a little more promising for me. It turned out that all my sweat during my weird rehab routine from last fall did produce some equity. Fully healed and in decent shape, I arrived on campus in August to start two-a-day practices and found out pretty quickly that I was at least in the mix to make the 18-man travel roster. It was exciting for me, but not a total surprise. I guess I felt that at this point, four years in, I'd be someone the coaches wanted on that roster, for experience if nothing else.

With Stolly gone, we had new leadership. Some of those guys who were freshmen on the last national championship team were seniors. Even with those seniors, the team still was in something of a transition and needed to get back on track after last year's mediocre performance. Leadership was going to be critical.

The season started kind of slowly when we lost the opener 2-1 to South Carolina then tied University of Virginia 1-1 in overtime. The encouraging news personally was that I was one of the first subs off the bench. About 15 minutes into the game, Coach Yeagley would call my number, and I'd come in as a midfielder. It was all about adding high-energy sparks and work ethic—a couple of my specialties. Playing with Pete, when the two of us were on the field together, was a ton of fun. Talk about high energy. And, I was pretty excited for another reason: I figured I was one step closer to the ultimate dream of starting.

After those first two games, we went on a bit of a roll, beating Notre Dame and Michigan State—marking our 45th consecutive game without a loss against a Big 10 team. Then we recorded three consecutive shutouts against Bowling Green, Ohio State, and Cincinnati.

Next up was a trip to Southern Illinois University-Edwardsville, always a big game for us. As off the radar as it was to most people, SIUE had a very competitive soccer program. This year the Cougars were nationally ranked.

A few minutes into the game, I was inserted on the outside midfield and was running down the field as teammate Timmy Hylla, a star who just a season before had taken time to tell me how much I'd improved, went in for a tackle against a big guy from SIUE then went crashing to the ground. Timmy broke his leg. Storm clouds rolled in. Lightning fired through the sky, and the game was cancelled.

We never made up that game and there is no report of it in official records, but it stays with me to this day. That night was the end

.

of Timmy's career, and it made me think about how precarious athletes' existences are.

As fans, we'll watch a game and see an athlete go down, hope for a few moments that everything will be fine then turn our attention right back to viewing the game almost before the athlete is carted or limps off the field. Then, in most cases, we forget the guy or girl. Watching Timmy go down and never really get back up was very tough for me, especially given what I'd been through the year before. But it was tough on a lot of the guys for much the same reason. It's heartbreaking to watch a friend suffer the end of a sport he embraced with every fiber of his body and lose such an important team leader. Beyond that, losing someone in that way—in the middle of a really intense game—shakes up everyone because we all know it could have been and may be any one of us at any given instant. You train yourself to avoid thinking about it because if you do think about it too much, you'll be far too tentative on the field and probably end up getting hurt. But underneath our seemingly laser focus and 110 percent effort on a sport, that tiny, frightening realization lingers. It's a rough sport. Much as we have all these rules to insure equality for teams, unfair things happen out there. We're one step, one twist, one collision away from the end of it all.

And, here's the other dramatic and uncomfortable aspect of Tim's injury. It opened the door for another player. Two days after the SIUE game, we hosted St. Louis University, another tough rival. Before warm-ups, coaches gathered us in the locker room to go through last-minute scouting on the Billikens, get us on track mentally, and announce the starting lineup.

"Okay, guys," Coach Yeagley said, "we're going to have Rod, Stoyanovich, and Shapert at forwards up top; at mids, we'll have JJ and Herb Haller." Then he paused and looked at me.

"And, Whitey," he said. "Whitey's starting at left mid. Dammit, he's earned it and we're proud of him. Congratulations, Whitey."

I felt goose bumps sweep over me. A couple guys—Pete was among them—slapped me on the back. A few others actually clapped, and I heard a whoop or two. They were genuinely excited for me, all of them, even Coach Yeagley. I actually got a little choked up. My fourth year in the program; all those times I was told I'd never make it; told to transfer; the injury that nearly ended everything. Here I was, a starter for the powerhouse Indiana University Hoosiers. I almost pinched myself to make sure I wasn't dreaming.

Coach Yeagley finished announcing the starters, and we walked from the locker room, crossed the street, and scaled the gentle asphalt incline to Armstrong Stadium. Flanked by Pete and John Johnson, JJ, my heart was hammering but I tried really hard not to show it. We had a game to play.

Then I saw my mom and dad, who were tailgating in the parking lot next to the stadium. My big brother Pete also happened to be there, which made the moment that much more powerful, except that I never got a chance to tell them.

As soon as she laid eyes on me, my mom started clapping her hands and hopping in place.

"You're starting today!" she shouted, beaming, and still clapping, but now it looked like she was dancing in place. "You're starting today!"

She was almost as excited as I was; more probably. Heck, she could have taken the field and scored at least once she was so juiced.

I found out later that one of the assistant coaches, Dan King, ran up the hill ahead of the team and told my parents. That's how much those guys cared for me and my family. It's a gesture, a moment that almost brings tears to my eyes to this day.

I felt ready to go, and I think Coach Yeagley was hoping that, by making me a starter, I'd inject a little electricity and passion in the on-field team chemistry. But, as hard as I'd worked and as ready as I thought I was, the whole thing was too much for me. I just was too nervous, and I let those nerves overtake me. Instead of playing the fired-up style that I'd exhibited before all this, I played a little tentatively. I remember thinking that I didn't want to blow this chance. I wanted to do everything right. I simply lost sight of the aspects of my game that made me the most valuable to my team. No big picture perspective. Too self-absorbed, I almost played out of fear. The result was that I was flat, didn't bring the fire that was my hallmark, and it indicated a larger, related problem with our team.

We lost 3-1, an embarrassing game that would have been 3-0 if Rod Castro hadn't scored with a little more than two minutes left in the game. That one goal said a lot about where our team psyche was. A handful of guys, mostly upperclassmen, celebrated the score as if it were a game-winner. And, I remember thinking two things: First, the underclassmen were watching, of course. What example were they seeing? Second, during the championship years, IU players never, ever, would have celebrated a goal to bring us within two. If anything, we would have grabbed the ball out of the net quickly, run it out to midfield, and jumped right back into action. To me that late goal against St. Louis was a microcosm of what was happening with our team that year. Something was missing. We had gotten off track. We played flat and against St. Louis, always a grudge match, that was inexcusable. Much as I loved the guys, individual objectives had replaced team goals. We all want to hit our individual goals, whether it's in sports, personal endeavors, or business. They're important to keeping a team motivated, but if we start to place too much emphasis on those and lose sight of the bigger picture, overall poor performance starts occurring and then settles in. Widespread misery typically isn't too far behind.

Coaches certainly picked up on the dynamic. They were so angry with our approach that they told us to take the next day off. No practice on Monday. They wanted us to clear our heads, and I think they needed to clear theirs as well.

So, after classes on Monday, a teammate, Dave Eise, and I went golfing. I love to golf, and Dave and I had a great time together, enjoying each other's company, laughing, getting a rare break from the grind. I felt like it really helped.

But Coach Yeagley had called an emergency team meeting while we were on the golf course. Cell phones didn't exist back then. So, Dave and I were absent. And, while we decompressed a little on the links, the team tried to regroup and zero in on the problems.

And, the major problem, Coach Yeagley told the team, was me. He pinned responsibility for two goals directly on me, and no one spoke up. Believe me I understand the circumstances. When a coach is in full rant mode, everyone is sort of keeping their head down, trying to avoid the gunfire. If the coach wanted to blame one guy for the loss, you're just grateful you're not that guy. That's about as far ahead as you look. You just hope to survive the meeting.

When Dave and I returned to campus, JJ gave us a recap of what happened: that Coach Yeagley was angry we'd missed the meeting and he was white hot at me. With the team gathered around, JJ recounted, Coach replayed film of the two goals he said were my fault, and pointed out why.

I was sick. Just couldn't believe what I was hearing, and kept asking JJ questions, trying to get more information, trying to get a feel for the atmosphere of the meeting. And, JJ tried to explain, but mostly shook his head.

"You're in big trouble, Whitey," JJ kept saying. "You're in the dog house. That's all there is to it."

I didn't know what to do. All these thoughts flooded my mind, and I was unable to make sense of them. I was angry at the team and coaches, felt like this was an unfair attack, like I'd been picked on. But I also was angry with myself. If I'd just gotten to the stinking meeting, maybe the coaches would have eased up a little. At least I would've had a chance to defend myself. Plenty of other things were going on in that game and with the team overall — mainly that we'd lost nearly all sense of camaraderie and a team-first approach, which led us to play very uninspired soccer. All that got glossed over because I was the easy target.

Plus, I was in a deep state of disbelief that my prospects had turned so quickly and so drastically. It was the proverbial 180 degrees — from nearly climbing to the top of the ladder to dropping in a free fall.

So, yeah, I was pissed, really pissed.

I had to come up with a strategy. One thing I wasn't going to do was show up for practice the next afternoon like nothing had happened. But I also didn't want to talk to teammates about it. They were going to be too kind and try to put a positive spin on it. Besides, all of us were riding in the same boat. We needed a bird's-eye view to see where we were on the ocean. I needed a reality check.

I called my brother Pete, who told me he didn't see what Coach Yeagley saw.

"You didn't play spectacular," Pete said, "but you didn't play that bad, either." Essentially, he told me he didn't think I hurt the team, and he couldn't pin blame for the two goals on me.

That was a little reassuring, but I still couldn't sleep. First thing Tuesday morning I called Coach Yeagley and said I needed to talk to him before practice. He agreed to meet. I remember thinking I was going to go in there and fire on him, tell him in no uncertain terms how I felt and why it was unfair to point all this blame at me.

When I walked in his office about 2 o'clock, he was seated at his big desk, two assistant coaches flanking him, a small projector near his elbow. I could feel the righteous courage drain from me, replaced by a surge of anxiety and agitation. I was losing my nerve.

I started by apologizing for missing the meeting. They acknowledged it but said nothing more. So, I went into my recollection of what I was told—that they'd pinned a lot of the blame for the loss on me, specifically two of the goals.

"I just wonder where you see that and how you think that happened," I said, my voice shaking.

"I'll show you," Coach Yeagley said.

He turned to the projector, which was pointed to the side wall. He flipped it on and started playing game film from a few seconds before one of the St. Louis goals. A Billiken player got to a ball a second or two before I did, moved past me, and scored. Coach Yeagley stopped the film, turned to me.

"You should have been able to get to the ball before the guy from St. Louis, Whitey. No two ways about it."

Then he forwarded the film to a few seconds before the next goal and replayed it.

"Same thing on this one, Whitey," Coach Yeagley said. "You should have gotten to that ball quicker."

"But, Coach," I said, "there was no way I could have gotten there any faster; no way I could have made up that ground."

"Whitey," he said, firmness in his voice, "it's right there on the film. You should have closed that distance. You needed to challenge that guy, slow him down at least." The other two coaches agreed.

I was silent while I listened to them pick me apart for a few more moments, and I thought for a second about bringing up everything else that was going on with the team. But it felt so wrong. I really liked my teammates and didn't want to attack them. That would have been really bad form and been seen as a petty defense mechanism from a cry-baby brat. That wasn't me. *Take responsibility,* I thought. *Don't blame others. Be a man.* Besides, I wasn't going to change the coaches' view, not today, not ever.

"You earned the start, Whitey," Coach Yeagley said. "That's why we gave it to you. And, we counted on you, but you didn't come through. It was a poor performance."

Going into the meeting, I was hoping we'd clear the air and that I'd achieve a little damage control, get them to see things at least a little from my perspective and still keep my chances alive.

Six minutes after I walked in, it was over, my mission a disaster. They gave me no clarity on where I stood and what would come next, which was their way of saying I was out—out of the starting lineup for sure and out of their plans altogether. Use whatever word you'd like. Insurmountable comes to mind. Kiss of death would be another fitting phrase. When I walked out of the office, two thoughts kept spinning in my head: First, I'd gotten my one opportunity and I freaking blew it; second, the coaches were thinking, *This is why we can't afford to take chances like this. We were right all along about you, Whitey. You're not good enough.*

Game after game, I rode the bench, never playing, never even getting a glance from Coach Yeagley. The doghouse was where I lived, and I was going to be there forever. Heck, I could've gotten a mortgage on the place. I kept working hard in practice but it seemed more pointless than ever. The entire atmosphere was pretty demoralizing, as demoralizing as I'd ever experienced. Everybody was passing me up, and the team was dividing into factions. Discipline was unraveling. During games, we were goofing off on the bench, and not just a little.

Throughout all this aggravation and dispiriting existence, one of the things that kept me going was my casual friendship with Pete Stoyanovich, who came to be called Stoyo.

It turned out that my first impressions of him were spot on. He was a really fun, down-to-earth guy who loved to laugh. I came to learn that we also had similar ethnic backgrounds. His was Macedonian, mine Greek, and that seemed to draw us closer. Like me, family was really important to Stoyo, especially his relationship with his mother. We shared the same sense of humor and the understanding that working hard could be fun. Over the months, we really enjoyed each other's company during practice. And, on the rare times I'd see him at a party or somewhere on campus, we'd seek each other out and always have a few laughs.

But that crazy schedule of his made it tough for us to hang out very much, and I think that hinted at something more. To many people, Stoyo looked like he had the world by the tail, and he did. How many college freshmen are the subject of a feature article in *Sports Illustrated?* He was an extraordinary athlete destined for the professional or Olympic ranks. Plus, he was one of the most likeable guys you could meet and had the good looks that would turn heads when he walked in a room.

Yet, because he split his time between the football and soccer teams, he wasn't firmly rooted in either. And, when he wasn't with one of those, he was rushing between the two teams or running around campus. The result, I think, was that he didn't have any really close friendships at IU. He was somewhat untethered; might have been a little lonely; and when his world exploded in October of 1986, I'm sure he felt very much alone, angry, and confused, but mostly overwhelmed with grief.

The team first got word of it on a Tuesday afternoon when we gathered for practice. Coach Yeagley announced that Stoyo was called home abruptly for personal reasons, and it was unclear when he'd return. Coach said nothing more and we were pretty confused because we didn't hear anything for a few days. Apart from being one of our best players, Stoyo was beloved by everyone on the team. His absence was palpable, and we all sensed that whatever the reason he went home it probably wasn't good.

It turned out that Stoyo tragically and abruptly had lost his mother, the person he was closest to throughout his life. He had no time to prepare for it. No time to say goodbye. She was just gone.

It's a curious thing about human nature. When real heartbreak happens to a person, the instinct for many is avoidance. We feel extremely awkward, even helpless. We don't know what to say. We don't want to upset the grieving person any more than he or she already is. All that's understandable, but I'm wired a little differently when it comes to those things, and I think the first time I recognized it was with Stoyo, with this wrenching loss he suffered.

Like I said, we weren't particularly close. I'd venture to say our friendship at the time was the same as probably dozens, maybe a hundred others, the guy had. When I heard about his mother's death, I, too, didn't know what to say or how to respond. I knew he'd be returning in a few days, and I didn't want to make the guy feel any more pain. I wanted to help him get through it, but I didn't want him to push aside or forget his mother. It all was so confusing. I felt totally unsure of myself.

But I knew this much: The guy needed somebody. He shouldn't be alone when he got back to campus, and I decided that the very least I could do was be there. That's it. Just be present for him. What I was going to do when he got there, I didn't know. Maybe six other people would be with him or waiting there for him. Maybe the guy would look at me like I was crazy. Maybe he'd tell me to leave him alone or completely ignore me. But I was going to be there.

So, I found out from Coach Yeagley when Stoyo was returning, got to his dorm, and waited in the hall outside his door for about an hour. It was Sunday night. The walkway was vacant. I still had no idea what I was doing.

When he showed up, he was alone. He wasn't perplexed by the sight of me. He wasn't angry. He wasn't uncomfortable. He unlocked the door to his room, set down his luggage, embraced me, and started sobbing, which is what I did.

I'm not sure what I said. I may not have said a word—didn't have to. All he wanted was for someone to be there, and that's all I did. I didn't know to do anything else. I really can't put into words what transpired in his room. It was a blur. It was overwhelming, and yeah, it was really painful. But it demonstrated something life affirming, too: the value of presence, and it was an epiphany for me. Sometimes all we need is each other. If we have that—if we know we have that authentic presence—we have something more resilient than our loss, something that enables us to carry on, to give us just enough strength to take that next step. I guess maybe that's what it came down to that night with my friend Stoyo. I was there for him and that, it turned out, was something he really needed.

From that moment, Stoyo and I were locked in to each other's lives. We shared a close, almost indescribable bond and started hanging out all the time. When we could arrange it, he'd come home to my parents' place with me, trips that occurred more often as time passed. He ended up being embraced by my entire family, establishing an especially warm relationship with my dad. We didn't grow to love Stoyo. We loved him immediately.

* * *

My soccer prospects were altogether different. I continued to ride the bench, not playing a minute for six, seven, eight games. But something changed inside me after my experience with Stoyo. Much as he might think I gave him support, he gave me something. I stopped worrying so much about my own troubles and started to think a little bigger. At the center of everything, I understood now more than ever that soccer is just a game; that, like many games, it can teach us a great deal about life. But it's a kids' game. Suddenly, my personal agenda of whether I'd play or not started to matter less. How did something like that measure up to what Stoyo was enduring? It made my worries seem like a mosquito bite.

I actually relaxed quite a bit, even surrendered in a way, and I started feeling better, liberated, almost empowered. That new perspective gave me something else: a broader view of our team, that bird's-eye view we needed. And, I wasn't all that crazy about what I saw.

After the St. Louis game, we won a game, then lost a game and then went on a nice run of three victories, helped in large part by Stoyo's scoring. But we really couldn't get on track. We tied Marquette in overtime and then went to Clemson—always a looming nemesis for us—for an invitational tournament where we'd play the Tigers on Friday night and American University on Sunday. It was make or break time for us. We had to put together a very strong finish to even have a shot at making the NCAA tournament. And, making the NCAA tournament was the absolute minimum acceptable performance for IU soccer. We'd made it nearly every season in the 32 years of NCAA soccer at Indiana.

The flight to South Carolina was really upbeat. We didn't fly that often, so when we did, it felt special and added a little extra spark of excitement. And Clemson had quickly become one of our top three or four rivals. They beat us in the 1984 NCAA final and beat us the next year at home in a prestigious early-season tournament. When they came to our place, our fans showed up in rowdy numbers, and we were expecting the same thing from their side. That got us jacked up even more.

Clemson didn't disappoint. Students were hanging out of dorm rooms shouting at us. During warm-ups, the speakers filled the stadium with George Thorogood's "Bad to the Bone." A big crowd was flowing in the bleachers. I felt like we understood the importance of the game and were ready to rock.

I was dead wrong.

We came out lifeless again. Guys were barking at each other. Our play was too improvised and lacked team continuity. It looked like it was every man for himself, and it looked very uninspired. It's one thing if your teammates are working hard and missing shots wide or not connecting on passes. It's entirely different if they don't give a darn and are pointing fingers.

Coach Yeagley knew what was going on, but I think he was at a loss for how to right the ship. At one point, he did glance down the bench at me and call my name to go in the game, which I did—I must admit—without much passion. He yanked me three minutes later, which I deserved, and I didn't play another minute.

On the bench, we were jacking around, and I was as guilty as anybody. A bunch of us benchwarmers slid to one end, leaving a big gap between us and the regulars. We joked with each other; said we didn't care if we got called to play or not, that we might not go in if Coach Yeagley called our name. It was bush league, 7th grade behavior that goes against everything I believe about supporting your team. It was another sign that we were veering out of control, that we'd lost focus and were giving up, from the best player on the pitch to the guy at the very end of the bench.

Underneath that goofing, I felt sick to my stomach. Aware of IU soccer's rich tradition and what the team was just two years earlier — how those guys handled themselves without prodding or coddling from coaches, how much pride they took in IU soccer and in playing their asses off and making sacrifices for each other, in feeding off each other's commitment and energy — I watched what was unfolding and was ashamed of myself. I'd thrown in the towel, too.

At halftime of that game, the coaches said very little, if anything. I remember we walked off the field down 1-0 and, even with half a game left, it felt hopeless. We just didn't have it. We went out and the Clemson crowd was on fire. So was their team. We caved and lost 3-1. Might as well have been 5-0.

That night, all of what was going on with our team sort of spilled over. Several of us were caught out at a restaurant after curfew. A couple of us — including me — got back a few minutes late; other guys were out quite a bit later. It's not like they were robbing a liquor store or anything. They were just out at a restaurant. Normally, that wouldn't be a big deal, but when a team is struggling like we were, team rules become a little more important.

Now, we were saying to heck with the rules. We were making our own rules. Instead of trying to pull closer together as a team, we were headed in the opposite direction. It looked like our collective thinking — and, again, I was guilty, too — was that none of this rules stuff matters.

Well, it mattered to Coach Yeagley. That Sunday morning in the pre-game locker room talk before we took the field against American University, I could see him reeling, trying to keep the train from going off the tracks any farther. He was very angry at the curfew violations and kept saying we have rules and they're made to be kept.

"We're instituting a new policy, right here and right now," he said finally. "From this moment on, indefinitely, through the rest of this season, the winter indoor season and into spring, we have a 10 o'clock curfew before games. In your rooms by 10 o'clock sharp."

He looked around the room.

"Anybody, *anybody,* caught out after that will be suspended. And, if it keeps up, well, don't test me, guys. You won't like the results. Have I made myself clear?"

Everybody acknowledged him, then Coach Freitag, an All-American at IU in the early 1970s and one of the guys who established the program's eminence and kept it going for a few years, stepped up to speak. He tried to rally the team around IU's soccer history.

"Guys," he said, "this isn't just about people in this room. It's a whole lot bigger. You're not just letting yourselves down, you're letting down everyone and everything that has been built here over all this time."

He talked about the pride of wearing the IU jersey, how hard it was to establish and carry on that pride and about the expectations and responsibilities that come with all that.

"Be proud to wear that jersey," he said, "and don't ever let that tradition down; don't let yourselves down; your teammates down. Don't let down all the guys who came before you."

He actually got a little emotional and started tearing up.

Around the locker room, I could see a few guys mocking him. And, frankly, I couldn't believe it. Coach Freitag had nailed it. He'd put all of it into perspective, reminded me and all of us what it takes to be a champion and how hard all those guys who'd come before us had worked to build something extraordinary from nothing and how they fully understood the sacrifices that must be made for a team to succeed at the very highest level. All the details matter if you want to be the best. You must continue to find ways to get better and help your teammates do the same. If you want to be mediocre, stay out after curfew and celebrate personal accomplishments over team objectives. If you want to be champions, work for your teammates harder than you've ever worked at anything else.

His talk woke me up. No matter what anybody else thought, I knew that something had to be done. I might not be able to rally all the guys, but I told myself that I at least could set an example, even if it was from the bench. My personal antics and lax attitude were over. When we stood to leave the locker room for the game against American, I knew I wasn't going to sulk and screw around while sitting out this game or any other. I was going to support my team. If my name was called to play with 30 minutes in a tie game or 30 seconds left in a 4-0 blowout, I'd run out there and play like a madman. I would honor all curfews and work hard in practice. I would do whatever I could to get our collective psyche back where it needed to be.

American was an average team that year, eminently beatable. As a matter of fact, I'd venture to say that if we had played them 10 times, we'd have won 9. But, after all that emotion in the locker room meeting, we came out and looked anemic. It was so disheartening; so aggravating.

At halftime, down 1-0, we trudged over to a shady tree near the field and sat in a loose circle, getting drinks and stretching. The coaches stood a few feet away, and I was sort of waiting for them to say something while I stewed. But they didn't, and I think that's because they were at wit's end. They could think of nothing more to say.

So I did.

I really had no right to do it. I wasn't a leader. Maybe I thought about how Stolly and Keith would view this season. Maybe I was still hearing the words of Coach Freitag, who I respected immensely, and was a little angry that he'd been ignored, even mocked. Whatever it was, I'd reached the boiling point and went with my instincts in the moment.

I stood and worked my way to the center of the circle. I could see guys staring at me, wondering what the heck I was doing.

I eliminated any confusion right away.

"Look," I said, "I know I sit on the bench. I've sat on the bench for four years, and I'm okay with that. You guys are better than me. I get it."

I started turning around so I could look at everybody.

"But here's the situation: It's one thing to sit on the bench and watch a team play hard, play for each other, and not reach expectations," I said. "But sitting on the bench watching you guys play is (*bleeping*) pathetic. It's embarrassing. It's insulting. That I will not stand for."

They were completely silent, coaches included. I think they must have thought I was nuts and maybe I was. I could feel the volume of my voice rise. My head seemed to fill with pressure.

"I cannot possibly sit there and watch that uninspired (*bleep*). The individual soccer that's being played out there? It's ridiculous. The laziness? It's got to end. Who in the (*bleep*) do you think you're playing for?"

Now, my voice was in full shouting mode, and I had everyone's attention. I was, as they say, in a zone.

"This is Indiana (*bleeping*) University, man! You're (*bleeping*) all over everything that guys like Coach Freitag and everybody before us has worked their asses off for. It's (*bleeping*) humiliating to have to sit there and watch it and even more (*bleeping*) humiliating to be associated with the (*bleep*) that I've been watching on the field. When are we going to get our heads out of our asses and start playing like a (*bleeping*) team, guys, like a team that IU can be proud of? It's getting a little late, don't you think?"

I went on like that for about a minute more. I don't cuss, not normally, but these were abnormal circumstances that called for a little emphatic language. I didn't name names, didn't single out examples of bad play. I just tried to convey that everyone was guilty and that we needed to come together. Then I stopped and stood there, somewhat unsure of what had just flowed from my mouth. I'd never done anything like that in my life.

Nobody mocked me. Everybody—players and coaches—were silent. You could hear the leaves rustle in the breeze; the birds chirp. The guys stood and made their way across the field to the bench for warm-ups. I stayed back a few feet to try and catch my breath, stop my vision from pulsating. A couple of teammates, John Trask and Herb Haller, came up, patted me on the back, saying words like "unbelievable, great job. We needed that."

I guess it worked, at least a little. We came out and played harder. As he would prove time after time on NFL gridirons for more than a decade, Stoyo stepped up in a pressure situation and scored a late goal, saving the day. The game ended in a 1-1 tie.

I didn't play a minute, which surprised me a little. But our post-season tournament hopes remained alive. That's what I cared about most. And, I think that game—specifically my halftime rant—may have been a turning point for me, although I was clueless at the time.

Next up was a trip to Evansville to play the Purple Aces, another challenging opponent, especially at their place. I had a decent week of practice but was given no indication that I'd play. It had been eight games of barking in the dog house. So, a couple days before the trip to Evansville, I persuaded my parents to miss it. They'd come to nearly all my games. They'd even wanted to come to the Clemson game all the way down in South Carolina, until I finally persuaded them against that one, too. I played so rarely that I felt selfish and a little foolish having them in the stands, much as they enjoyed hanging out with the team and other parents—and much as those people loved hanging out with my fun-loving mom and dad. When I reminded them that Evansville is a three-and-a-half-hour drive from their house, that the game was on a Sunday afternoon, and that I wasn't going to play, they finally relented.

And, of course, I played; I played a key role, as a matter of fact.

Whenever we were at Evansville, fans packed the field, even standing close to the sideline, and got pretty raucous. This game was the same thing, and I loved it. But our team, unfortunately, again fell into one of our uninspired funks and went down 1-0 with about 20 minutes to play. Coach Yeagley called to Marc Behringer and Kenny Godat, a couple of guys who'd played throughout the year, to sub in the game. Coach must have been really desperate because then he turned to the end of the bench and called my name, too. I was startled, to say the least, but jumped up and began getting warm. With something like 15 minutes left, he inserted the three of us in the game, shouting at us to "make something happen."

None of us were big scorers, but we went in with some passion and some fire, and I could feel the energy level on our team intensify. Over the years, I'd kind of established myself—as much as a benchwarmer can—as a scrapper, a highly- competitive, slightly feisty guy with a motor that always ran at high RPMs. Some might even call me a pest, and they'd be pretty darn accurate. Lovable pest is the way I like to think of it.

Late in the game, John Trask took a shot from about 30 yards out, and if there's one thing I'd become somewhat proficient at it's looking for shots off loose balls and rebounds. A guy or girl can score a fair number of goals if he or she charges the net on every shot, controls any rebound or ricochet, and punches it at the net. I recorded more than a few goals that way.

In this case, JT's shot bounced off the goalkeeper's chest and skidded about six feet in front of him. I'm crashing the goal like a rocket toward that ball. Nothing's going to stop me from pouncing on it.

Except that the goalkeeper got there an instant before I did and I inadvertently—and it was inadvertent—kneed him in the head. It hurt. I know because my knee throbbed and tingled. But I honestly did not hit the guy on purpose. I might be a competitive—lovable—pest, but I would never carry it that far.

The keeper went down and was hurt, not enough to come out of the game, but his bell was rung. The crowd erupted, and one of the Evansville players near the goalkeeper was highly displeased with my play, expressing his discontent to me in very colorful and descriptive terms. He thought I took a cheap shot, and when I jogged by him, heading toward my midfield position, he took my legs out completely from me, or tried to.

The refs noticed, blew the whistle and gave us a penalty kick. Chris Keenan stepped up, buried the ball in the back of the net, and IU tied the game at 1-1, which is how regulation ended. A momentum shift had occurred. The crowd was silent then agitated. Overtime was ready to start. A whole lot of energy was crackling among our team, and I was at the center of it. I liked that feeling.

Before the overtime, Coach Yeagley pulled us about 10 yards into the field to go over a few things, let us catch a breather, and get some water. He was keeping me in the game, which made sense but also made me very excited. I'll never forget what happened next.

The crowd was in that between-periods lull and silent. Coach Yeagley had just finished briefing us when a woman—sounded like a college girl—shouted:

"We love you, Whitey!"

Everybody heard it but couldn't acknowledge it; we had to stay focused, so I didn't know who said it and never found out. I did know that my mom wasn't in the crowd, so it couldn't have been her. And, if I had found out who'd said it, I would have told her this: I love you, too. Your burst of enthusiasm remains one of the most exciting, heartfelt memories of my soccer journey. Thank you.

The double-overtime game ended in a tie, and our tournament hopes were alive. The bus ride home was euphoric. I couldn't wait to get back to call my folks and tell them all about the day. But, just like when I got my start against St. Louis, they already knew.

On their way home, two or three parents who had attended the game pulled off the road to call my folks from a pay phone—remember, cell phones didn't exist back then—to tell them what a terrific game I'd played. When I finally did call them Sunday night all breathless, my mom and dad were telling me details I didn't even know. It was weird and hilarious. While I was bummed that I'd kept my folks from the game, I was really touched by the gestures of those other parents. So were my mom and dad. It showed again just how much everybody cared about them and me. It was almost better for them than being there.

That week our practices were crisp, and we were excited about our chances in a tournament in Tampa on the final weekend of the regular season. Just maybe we were going to put together a strong final two games that would generate a little momentum as the post-season tournament began and push us to a deep run. Deep runs in the tournament were—and are—a standard expectation for IU men's soccer. Like I've said, we gun for a national championship every year and have the horses to do it. The mood on the plane flight down was upbeat, focused. We knew we had to win both games in Florida to make the tournament, and we figured we could do it.

But again, once we took to the field, we played flat. I got in for a few minutes in each contest and tried to amp up the electricity, but we just didn't have it. We lost both games.

The plane ride back was silent, melancholy. We knew the only way we'd make the post-season tournament was on IU's reputation, not for our play.

That reputation wasn't enough. When tournament teams were announced, the Indiana Hoosiers were conspicuously absent, the first time that happened in a decade. In fact, IU teams had failed to make the tournament only twice before in the 32-year history of IU soccer. We also were the only team in IU history to fall short of 10 wins. Our final record was 9 wins, 6 losses, 4 ties. A certain downward spiraling momentum was building in the program. We'd gone from winning national championships in 1982 and 1983 to losing in the final in 1984, to losing early in the 1985 post-season tournament to getting aced out of the tournament altogether in 1986.

Then things got worse. Team dissent carried into the off-season. We had more disciplinary problems. Some guys were caught drinking and carousing, and Coach Yeagley took a tough stance. By the time it all got sorted out, three of our top players were gone. And, JJ, who had not been part of the shenanigans, transferred to play at St. Louis University, in his hometown, to be closer to his ailing father. On top of that, we lost two regulars to graduation. That made six; six of our best, most highly-recruited athletes were done playing at IU.

It was almost like somebody had driven a truck through the center of the team photo. We couldn't be sure if the program had hit rock bottom or was still falling. I felt like Coach Yeagley didn't know which way was up or how we were going to overcome this.

And, yet, deep inside, I looked at the scraps we had and felt a little spark of possibility. Maybe this moment was created for a reason, I thought. Maybe now, finally, was my chance to take everything that had stood in my way on this journey and use it to build a dream.

The persistent optimist had one season left to find out.

We had some reason to be hopeful as we headed into my final year.

7

*Being named Captain
was a great honor.*

CAPTAIN WHITEY

CHAPTER 7:

CAPTAIN WHITEY

Stoyo and I sat in Nick's, a popular campus hangout, a few days before two-a-day practices were to start. It was early August and few students had arrived on campus. We had been in contact a bit with other teammates over the summer and their general consensus was skepticism. He and I went to dinner to reconnect and talk about this year.

"I don't know, Whitey," Stoyo said. "We're missing a lot of difference-makers."

I had to agree. After the upheaval of last season, our team, figuratively speaking, looked a little like a bombed out building. From a manpower standpoint, from a talent standpoint, from a leadership standpoint, we were in bad shape, uncertain at best. You lose six thoroughbreds from a team—even one that had underachieved—and you're decimated.

Sitting there munching on pizza, my mind went back to the spring season when a few of the recent alums had returned and a couple of seniors set to graduate were hanging out with the team. One day after practice, while we were sitting around, they talked to me about our prospects for 1987.

A senior looked over the upcoming schedule, which was another typically rugged one for us, and went through it opponent by opponent.

"You're going to lose that one and that one," he said. "You'll probably tie this one. You'll lose that one, win this one…"

By the time he'd gotten to the end of the schedule, he had a somber prediction.

"You're gonna win five games," he said. "Gonna be a long season for you guys, Whitey."

Other recent alums sitting around agreed. I didn't say anything. Going into the 1987 season, we were untested, unsteady, and largely unfamiliar with each other, which made for a slightly scary scenario, especially when you consider that every one of our opponents always ramps up their game against us. Knocking off Indiana University is a badge of distinction, what's called a *statement win* for every team who faces us. It elevates their program's status big time. For some, beating us makes their season a success. And many of those opponents were aware of our vulnerability this year. They'd have a little extra confidence in gunning for us.

But I remember not being all that pessimistic after the gloomy predictions. In fact, I was a little inspired by the challenge of what was ahead of us. It was weird. I was calm. I thought maybe the purging of players was cleansing for us, and I tried to point out to Stoyo at least a few reasons to be a little optimistic.

"We still have some competitors," I told him, "guys who definitely could play top-caliber ball, if they want to bad enough."

I started naming them. Stoyo, who lead the national team in scoring a few years earlier and was our leading scorer last season, certainly was one. We also had Sean Shapert, a great playmaker, and Herb

Haller, a really skilled midfielder. Han Roest was a ball-winner type of guy in the midfield, and returning wingback Dave Eise was one of the quickest guys in the country.

Other factors were in play. Entering my fifth and final season I'd shed all my doubts about coming to IU. Stoyo's situation, like I said, gave me enormously valuable perspective. And, during our dinner, he indicated this might be his last year in soccer. The grind of playing two sports was taking its toll on him, and the National Football League had shown some early interest. I completely understood his mindset and thought if this is going to be his and my last season, I was going to do everything possible to make it memorable for both of us. I'd also gotten a boost at the end of last season when I received the team's Mental Attitude Award, given to the player whose work ethic and overall approach exemplified what the program strived for every year.

The result was that I became more relaxed and committed. I wasn't going to wring my hands about this decision to go to IU. I wasn't going to transfer. I wasn't going to quit the team. How could I do anything but see this through at this point? What an epic experience I'd had. Ending it all now seemed foolish, short-sighted, and sort of petty, like walking out of a really engaging movie before it ends. I was pretty fascinated by how this wild ride was going to turn out. The way I looked at it was I had my final year of IU soccer ahead of me, and I was going to make darn sure I got the most out of it. Almost like going down with my guns blazing.

During the spring season, I'd gotten back to my grinder status. I was looking to bring a lot of energy and try to make it a little contagious. I was pretty vocal and upbeat and encouraging. I tried to communicate to all the guys that we had a chance to do something special, maybe turn this thing around.

But at my evaluation at the end of the season, the coaches were very uncertain. I remember sensing that they were really unsure about the bold moves they'd made and all the ripples those might cause. I think they were nervous about how perceptions of what had happened at IU would affect recruiting, whether the upheaval would make it much more difficult to persuade the precious few very elite high school players to come to Indiana. It's a pretty delicate balance at that level. If IU failed to get those elite players, the program was going to decline. I think the coaches worried about the possibility of a lengthy descent, that IU could be digging out of this situation for 3-5 years and, once that happened, could any premier program recover? It was especially painful to think about because Coach Yeagley had toiled for so many years to build this program from nothing. He created it.

My personal evaluation wasn't personal at all. No analysis of my skills. No talk about where I might fit. It was brief, and they barely mentioned my name.

"What we need from you, Whitey," Coach Yeagley said, "is to come back in shape and be ready to go. Just be ready. We just don't know how it's all going to play out."

Over the summer, the coaches must have kept thinking about things and decided, finally, that I had some value. I was at home one afternoon eating lunch and got a surprise phone call from Coach Yeagley.

"Whitey," he told me, "we want to reward you for your effort, for everything you've done for the program."
    "Okay Coach," I said, unsure exactly what was coming, although I liked the sound of it so far.

"Coaches and I, we've freed up some money and we'd like to award you a scholarship."

I didn't know what to say. Up to this point, I'd been feeling like little more than an afterthought, not quite a throwaway guy, but close. Now, unexpectedly, coach was telling me I was an integral part of this team, that they really needed me. At least that's the way I viewed it.

I did what came naturally. I thanked him. Then I thanked him again. And again. I lost track of how many times I thanked him over the course of a 5-minute conversation, but it might have gotten into the double figures.

I could tell he was really proud to have given me that chance. And I told him I wouldn't let him down, that I'd show up for two-a-days in the best shape of my life. The confidence he showed in me, by giving me the scholarship, really resonated as the summer went on and got me jacked to work out that much harder. There is no better feeling than being wanted somewhere, and now, I definitely felt wanted as an IU soccer player.

The part that meant so much to me was that Coach Yeagley didn't have to do it. He knew I was coming back no matter what and that I was going to be as fired up as ever, with or without scholarship money. But he did it and that was an incredibly meaningful gesture on his part, one that gave me and my parents enormous pride in the sacrifices we had made. They also didn't mind breaking free from a semester's worth of tuition, books, room, and board.

The scholarship was the second signal that a certain momentum was building in my life. I was mostly clueless about it back then, but now it's clear that events had begun to move in a very distinct direction.

A few weeks earlier, near the end of the semester in May, Sherri Seger, my secret crush, called to see if my roommates and I were going out. Sherri and I had become friends by that time, hanging out with the same group of 10 or 15 people. But I'd long gotten over thinking that I had a chance of dating her. And I was okay with that. She was a really friendly, warm, upbeat person who was a pal and great fun to be around.

That night, with the semester coming to a close, fewer and fewer people were left on campus. JJ, Stoyo, and I were still around, and JJ and Stoyo are two of the most fun guys you want around at the end of a semester, or in the middle of the semester, or on a Tuesday at 10:37 a.m. They're just year-round fun, JJ and Stoyo. It helped that JJ, our roommate Rod Craig, and I had an apartment that was about as ideal as a college apartment could be: close to campus, really roomy, fairly stylish décor inside with a balcony overlooking a pool, and a stereo system that was loud enough to entertain the entire apartment complex.

"Yeah, JJ and Stoyo and I are going out," I told Sherri.

"Cool," she said. "Me and a friend of mine are looking to hang out. Let's all go together."

Sounded like a highly workable plan to me. We hit Jake's, a pretty lively college bar with a stage for live music, a dance floor, and seating throughout. Jake's was a versatile place, which is why we hung out there. You could sit and enjoy the music, dance and enjoy the music, or sit and enjoy the company. We did a little of all three that night, but the three of us—Stoyo, JJ, and I—we love to dance. Stoyo was about as smooth as they get, and JJ would prep the night by showing me a few new dance moves—moves he made up—prior to us heading out. It was something JJ did on a regular basis and tonight was no different.

"Voyage," a local 80s cover band, was playing that night. Once they broke into their first set, playing songs like "I'm Looking for a New Love," by Jodi Whatley, "Been Around the World," by Lisa Stansfield, and the band's own hit, "Strange Situation," we knew it was going to be a night of dancing. Sherri loved to dance, which made it that much more fun, and the place wasn't very crowded. So, our little group nearly had the entire dance floor to ourselves. We danced, laughed, told stories, reminisced, just had a blast. It was one of the greatest nights of my college life.

We all ended up back at our apartment, talking and laughing, listening to tunes. I found myself sitting next to Sherri on the couch, the two of us talking long after everyone else had left and gone to sleep. We talked all night. Conversation comes easy to me, and I'm generally interested in others. The funny thing was that even though Sherri and I had known each other for a couple years, I'd never really had the chance to have a long, in-depth conversation with her, something I loved to do with all close friends. Tonight, finally, we did. We talked about her past—having a choice of a gymnastics scholarship at IU or a track scholarship from University of Louisville, about when she broke her ankle during a meet and basically was forced to end her gymnastics career, about her likes and dislikes, about anything and everything you can imagine. It was fantastic. The conversation and laughter really flowed. And, as we talked, I was becoming more and more attracted to her character, to who she was, not just by her external beauty. My feelings over the past two years were being validated as the conversation went on. At one point, I looked out the balcony window and saw the first glow of sunrise in the distance. Sherri was getting up to leave. I thought I was at a moment, and I decided to take a chance.

I told Sherri Seger how I really felt about her. Then I kissed her. And she kissed me back. And it was good.

She smiled and went back to her apartment—we lived in the same complex—and I went to sleep, pretty pleased with myself. But I woke the next morning and all that confidence had evaporated. I thought I'd gone too far, that I'd ruined a great friendship by taking things in a direction they shouldn't have moved. I kept asking myself what the heck I was thinking last night. *I should have just left things the way they were, with a wonderful night of conversation. Why did I have to push it by kissing her?* I was worried, angry, embarrassed, and really nervous about seeing Sherri the next time. I thought she'd probably cringe at the sight of me, and I'd feel like a real jackass.

I went out to the balcony that warm, spring afternoon to clear my head and there, at the pool with her friends, was Sherri. I froze for a second. *Awkward*, I thought. *Very awkward.*

She didn't think so. She flashed that electric smile and waved.

"Hey, Whitey," Sherri called. "Come on down and lay next to us."

I could hear the little man in my brain say, "Huh?" I wanted to look over my shoulder to be sure she was talking to me.

"Whitey," she shouted again. She was waving one arm, smiling wider now, patting the lounge chair next to her with the other. Did I see her giggle with her friends? "Come on down."

High five.

"Be right there," I said and went back inside. After doing a quadruple fist pump, I changed into my swim suit in world record time and headed to the pool.

What a day that was—the highest of highs and the lowest of lows. Really exciting but agonizing, too. I'd finally gotten to know the woman of my dreams. A relationship was developing, the kind of relationship that makes a red-blooded American boy like me very enthusiastic. But the semester was over. I was heading home for the summer and Sherri was staying in Bloomington for school. I couldn't believe the timing. I decided to stay another night. We went out with a few friends again, and again found ourselves engrossed in conversation. At the end of the night, I gave Sherri my parents' phone number and said if she ever wanted to come up for a visit, that I'd love to see her, and so would my parents.

But, in my heart, I thought it was over. When we said our goodbyes, Sherri and I left the relationship sort of open, and I knew what that meant: a long-distance romance that would unravel. I packed and left the next morning, trying to convince myself—and failing—that at least I'd gotten to know her and she was exactly the caliber of person I thought she was, better even. No matter what I told myself, though, what I knew was that a woman like Sherri wasn't going to be left alone on a college campus, even if it's the sleepy summer semester. She'll forget about me in a week, I thought, and I started listening over and over to a song Smokey Robinson released at the time, "Just To See Her," a soulful ballad that shot right to my heart.

Except it didn't happen the way I thought it would. Ten days after we said goodbye, Sherri called and invited me down to Bloomington for the weekend. *How about that?* I thought. *Whitey was still in the game, and that's all Whitey needs.* But there was one little hitch: My parents were having a big party the same weekend. I asked if she'd come up for that.

"Sure," she said.

You might already have gathered that my family has something of a reputation for being, shall we say, fun-loving. Growing up, our house was the place where all my friends and the friends of my three brothers and sister would hang out and the place where my parents routinely would throw parties. The door was always open. Maybe it's our Greek heritage, but we thrive on having people around us, often in big groups. My dad tells great stories that keep people in stitches, and he likes to get things rolling by playing German marching band music. It's a curious taste for a guy who's 100 percent Greek, but what the heck. Works for him. My mom's a great cook and a lively, sincere hostess who laughs at all his jokes and will lead the group in Greek dancing at the drop of a hat. I have wonderful memories of the gatherings we've had at our house. So do about 1,500 other people.

But, we can be overwhelming for "outsiders," and I was a little nervous Sherri might be intimidated by the Full Kapsalis Experience. She wasn't. She fit right in and we had a great time, an absolute riot, telling stories, laughing and staying up all night. She came up almost every weekend after that, and it was official. Whitey and Sherri were dating. High five, indeed.

The other wonderful thing that happened during that summer was my re-reintroduction to church. I'd been raised in a spiritual household but, like many people in their late teens and early 20s, had drifted to a somewhat apathetic place. Sherri attended regularly, and we made going to mass part of our Saturday night or Sunday morning routine when she'd come to my folks' place. When she was unable to come up for the weekend, I'd go to church alone.

It reopened a door to me. Today and for years now, my faith in God, my regular attendance in church, and my daily ritual of prayer and other involvement in my church are as vital to me as the blood that runs through my veins. My foundation in faith was built years before, but the physical act of attending church that summer brought that faith back to a prominent place in my consciousness, my heart, and soul and started me up a path that has been illuminating, fulfilling, and remarkable. I may put off some people for saying this, but it's true: The Good Lord guides me in virtually every step I take, has taught me so much, and is at the very center of my existence. I lean on Him for issues large and small, and He is always there. For that, I'm deeply and eternally grateful.

Late in the summer, just a few days before returning to campus, I got another boost. Sherri and her family invited me to spend the first week of the month with them in Hilton Head, South Carolina, where they gathered every year. I was a little nervous about getting derailed from my training, especially since soccer two-a-days started in mid-August, and I called Coach Yeagley to clear it with him. He gave me his blessing and it turned out to be perfect timing. Sherri's family was a bit more reserved than mine—just about everybody's family is a bit more reserved than mine—but they were warm, fun-loving people. And Sherri, being a collegiate athlete, fully understood the importance of what I was trying to do. She helped me with my stretches and made sure I ran on the beach every morning. After that, I'd go off on my own to juggle and dribble the soccer ball for an hour. Then I'd kick it around a little with some local kids who could play. I stayed vigilant about my nutrition. In the end, I probably worked out more down there than I would have at home. But what made it that much more powerful for me was my mental state. I was so comfortable and ecstatic being with Sherri. We were a great fit, a real team, and the trip wound up being a wonderful balance of relaxation and preparation a few days before the pre-season.

By the time I sat in Nick's eating pizza with Stoyo back in Bloomington, I was definitely in the best physical and emotional shape of my life. That probably was why I was a little more upbeat about our prospects.

"Maybe if we can just clear our heads and rally around each other," I told Stoyo, "we could make something special happen, turn things around."

Stoyo looked at me, and I couldn't read what he was thinking. In truth, I really wasn't sure what to expect, but I knew this much because I'd seen it develop in previous years: team chemistry and camaraderie can go a long way. Teams that win typically have intangibles that allow them to enjoy success, even if overall star-power is not there. I thought we had a chance—maybe very slight, but still a chance—of making a run if we could start liking each other and get back to playing IU soccer: team-oriented, self-sacrificing, aggressive, high-energy soccer.

And I figured the best way to do that was to show it myself, the proverbial lead by example, some of which I'd done during spring season. Going into our two-a-days, I'd decided I was going to assert my standing as the veteran who'd been in it for the long haul, even if it was from the end of the bench—a guy who bled IU crimson and was proud to put on the jersey. I was going to be the consummate teammate and the consummate coach's player. I was going to live by the rules and play by the rules. Don't get me wrong. I had my share of fun—I wouldn't be Whitey if I didn't know how to have a few laughs—but when it came to demonstrating what was needed to play at a premier level of soccer, I was going to be all business, and hope for the best.

The night after Stoyo and I met for dinner, we had our first team meeting in the lounge at Assembly Hall. I sat there sort of sizing up the players, wondering who my competition might be and where I might fit. I saw a lot of new faces, and I was thinking: Here I am, a fifth-year senior, still uncertain what my role would be. I was pretty sure I'd be one of the top 18 players who travel with the team. But beyond that, who knew?

Coach Yeagley called the meeting to order and, after running through some preliminaries, shook up things right away.

"For the first time in history," he announced, "I decided I'm going to name the team captains for the season before we even get started."

That got everybody's attention. The tradition at IU was for the team to complete two-a-days, and then the players would vote on who would serve as captains. It was an honor, obviously, but you had to earn it through the sweat and toil of those early practices, which always were grueling. Captains had to be guys who exemplified from head to toe what it took to be IU soccer champions—guys like my former roommates, Stolly and Keith, who'd been captains.

"And this year, coaches and I have decided on two guys," Coach Yeagley said, "who exemplify what leadership is all about here."

The room was dead silent. No one breathed. It felt like the air had been lifted from it.

"Bruce Killough," Coach Yeagley said.

That made perfect sense. Bruce was an All-American and member of the U.S. National Team in high school. An all-business guy who followed the rules and didn't drink or cat around late, Bruce was vocal, well-liked, and a workhorse. Most importantly, he placed the team ahead of everything else, all the time. The more I thought about it, he was an ideal choice for captain.

And then Coach Yeagley pointed in my direction. I felt something in my chest jump.

"And, Whitey," he said. "Whitey Kapsalis."

I was stunned speechless, overwhelmed. I could see Coach Yeagley's mouth move, and I heard the words "doing things right," "integrity," "character," "role model," "congratulations," but my head was spinning so fast and pounding so hard, I wasn't processing all of it.

First, I get the woman of my dreams. Next, I return to my faith. Then I get the scholarship. Now this. When was I going to wake up?

I wouldn't. This was my reality, and I was thrilled. Once I'd caught my breath and the meeting progressed, I looked around the room and grinned. Here we were, a team of relative unknowns being led by an All-American-caliber goalie and me, the kid who would never play at IU, the kid who was told to transfer, the kid who lost an entire season—and almost a career—to injury. This was going to be rich.

I rushed back to my apartment and called my parents and Sherri. They, of course, were beyond exuberant; they were so genuinely overjoyed for me—I swear I could hear my mom dancing—that it nearly brought tears to my eyes. When I hung up the phone, I couldn't help but sit there for a few moments and shake my head at what an unpredictable, fascinating journey life can be. What places we can go if we just open ourselves to the possible and get after it with everything we can give.

Now, it was time to get down to the real work, to tap into all that I'd been given from everyone—my parents, my brothers Danny and Pete, Pat McGauley, Stolly and Keith, of course; Stoyo, Mike "Mickey" McCartney, Coach Freitag, even Coach Yeagley—all those people who took the time with a kid who didn't stand out at all but just wanted a chance and was willing to work hard for it. I was ready, readier than I'd been for anything in my life.

Two-a-days started the next morning and, as you might guess, I was a little fired up. So fired up in fact, that I set a personal best—11 minutes and 34 seconds—in the notorious two-mile run that marks the first morning of two-a-days. I finished third behind a couple of guys who could run like deer. But I think I made the point and set the agenda early: We were going to push ourselves harder than ever before. We were going to be tougher than everybody else, and we were going to play with enthusiasm for each other as a true team. This year was it for me. It was all I had left. I was going to show them how it's done and how to make this one a memorable ride. Time to get after it, boys.

As the days passed, I was looking for something more to pull the team together, which I thought was extremely important after the implosion the year before. I remembered how music can be such a unifying force, and a popular tune of the time, Steve Winwood's "Back in the High Life Again," clicked in my head. Those of a certain age probably can remember. It's a song that's pretty well summed up by the title. The chorus is: "I'll be back in the high life again. All the doors I closed one time will open up again. I'll be back in the high life again. All the eyes that watched me once will smile and take me in."

Seemed like the perfect theme song for us that year. Stick with this and we're going to get IU soccer back where it belongs. I started playing the song sporadically in the locker room before practices. As the season wore on, it became a regular selection before games as well.

Music was one unifying theme, but I also wanted to be sure the guys were having fun. Nothing like a few laughs to bring people closer and take a little of the pressure off. Sure, we were going to have to work our asses off, but we could enjoy ourselves, too. So I tried to inject humor wherever I could.

I used one of my favorite stunts during daily stretches at practice, which a team captain is supposed to lead. But anybody who knew me knew I had zero flexibility. Me leading the team in stretches was like me leading them in Suzuki violin lessons. So, I embraced it and came up with the Whitey Stretch, which was bending at the hips, touching the knees with the fingertips then standing up straight and shaking it off. The boys liked that one, and we started making it part of our routine. Another favorite was the straight leg, in which you would lie on your back, flatten one leg on the ground, then grab the bottom of the foot in the air and straighten that leg, forming a 90-degree angle with the leg on the ground. My 90-degree angle was more like a bent knee 37 1/2 degrees. Lastly in the Whitey stretching regime was the butterfly stretch, in which we sat cross-legged, leaned forward, pressed our elbows against our knees, and gently flattened them to the ground, except that my knees refused to flatten—not even close, really. It almost looked like I was mocking some yoga pose, which I wasn't but was, sort of. Our head trainer would just watch and laugh. As long as I wasn't getting hurt, I guess he had to accept the fact that I just couldn't do it.

Two-a-days continued, and the early pre-season ratings of college soccer teams from *Soccer America* magazine came out. Here's the funny and telling thing about where we stood: In the first pre-season poll, we appeared as No. 12 in the nation, but coaches throughout the country made so much of an uproar, contending that the ranking was based on nothing but history, we were dropped from the rankings altogether the next week. We hadn't even played a game, and we'd fallen out of sight. It was a very strange, unsettling experience. We knew we were an uncertain commodity but that turn of events was almost laughable.

For the first time in anybody's memory, IU not only wasn't in the top 5 or 10, it wasn't even in the top 20. We were a nonentity. Unranked. Unknown. It was shocking for a program that by then had racked up two national championships in recent years and been to the final four more than a dozen times. The big dogs had become the underdogs, but I had to admit, something about that role appealed to me. Imagine that—me being captain of an underdog team.

Practices, though, started revealing that this team might be better than we thought. We had a real surprise show up in Kenny Snow. He was an incoming freshman from Schaumburg, Illinois who we had hoped might help us right away—a somewhat unusual expectation from a program that had always been so deep and rich in upperclassmen talent. In practices, he was scoring goals like crazy. Regardless of the drill, shooting exercises, 1 v 1 drills, and scrimmages, the guy was putting the ball in the back of the net all the time.

Still, something was bothering me. Although I was a captain, my playing time was not what you might expect for a captain. During drills, we worked out as one large group, but as we got deeper into the practices, coaches started separating starters from nonstarters. It's a little subtle to the untrained eye, but I picked up right away how teams were being divided, and I noticed that I kept being shuffled off to the nonstarting squad, the second string, during scrimmages. It was clear the coaches still didn't believe I had the talent to play at that level. They were going to bench me.

I waited it out for a week but things didn't change. During that time, I kept thinking, *What kind of a captain can I be if I'm not a starter?* I'd never heard of a captain who came off the bench, unless he was injured, and had to limit his playing time. The captain was supposed to be a leader, and leaders needed to be on the field of battle. This was another time when Sherri helped. We would talk for hours every night, and hearing her calm, confident voice eased my anxiety immensely and helped keep me focused and optimistic.

Finally, though, the frustration became too much, and I approached the coaches after practice one day. I can remember it very clearly. We'd finished the second of our two-a-days. It was about 5 o'clock, the hottest time of what had been our fifth consecutive day of sweltering conditions. Tables were set on one end of the field, and on top of those were coolers of water. Guys were chugging water and shedding their cleats, socks, and shin guards for flip flops. Coach Yeagley was standing nearby. Assistant Coach Don Rawson was sitting on a table. We'd had another lively practice, and I decided this was a casual enough moment to approach the coaches.

"Coach, can I talk to you for a minute?" I said.

"Sure, Whitey," Coach Yeagley said. "What is it?"

"Well, you know I respect you and as your captain, I'll do everything you guys want me to do, from the bench or wherever. But I've got to level with you. It's going to be tough to be captain from the sidelines. I could have a much greater impact on the field. And, I would really appreciate it if you would just pay attention for the next three or four days to what I'm doing in practice, out on the field, to my ability today, not what it was three or four years ago when I showed up as a mangy walk-on who would never play. Just keep an eye on things when I'm out there and give me an honest shot."

What I remember most about that four-minute exchange was that I was calm, confident, and respectful. It was the polar opposite of nearly every other conversation I'd had with the coaches, especially my anxious, twitchy evaluations.

They agreed to give me a long look, and I knew it was hard for them. I realized that while I was probably one of the most well-liked guys on the team with the right attitude and work ethic, the coaches still saw me as the kid who never would play at IU.

Well, I must have made them think. Three days later, we had our first scrimmage against another team I was somewhat familiar with, University of Southern Indiana, at home. I started and had a real strong game, in fact. But I nicked up my knee after running into the goalie at the end of the game, and I missed a couple days of practice. The next weekend, we were scheduled to play in the IU Classic, a tournament that kicks off the regular season and always brings to Bloomington the top programs in the country—schools like Duke, North Carolina, Virginia, UCLA, Clemson, and South Carolina. It's a big weekend, when games draw as many as 4,000 fans. Playing in The Classic is one of those milestones, one of those markers in an IU soccer player's career. In previous years, I played 5 or 10 minutes throughout all The Classics. But this year was supposed to be different.

Except that Coach Yeagley came up to me in the locker room a few minutes before announcing the starting lineup in the first game and told me I wasn't starting because of the injury. I was crushed and not entirely sure I believed him. I still think the coaches had that lingering feeling that I was beneath the skill level of the IU program. We lost to South Carolina 3-1 and then won a close one, 2-1, against Southern Methodist University, and the tournament was over. I played maybe 15 minutes. Really disappointing.

But, I hung in there. Like I said, I was in this for the long haul, and I'd hung in through plenty of other tough times. It was what I did best. I'd just have to hang in through some more. The knee got better, and we came out strong the next game with a 6-0 shellacking of Michigan State, which was a great feeling. I didn't start but I did come off the bench and played some significant minutes. Winning as handily as we did proved my point that IU was a dominant program and that this journey was well worth it. I would rather have never played at IU than have come to Bloomington for Michigan State and get beat 6-0.

Still, we weren't really playing cohesively, and the coaches were getting increasingly agitated. In our next game at Notre Dame, we missed a penalty kick late and lost 4-3 in overtime. It was a particularly galling defeat for the coaches. They and we viewed Notre Dame as a heated, in-state rival but a team we almost always handled pretty well. In fact, we'd never lost to them before that game. I played very little and my pride was hurt, especially since a high school buddy of mine in grad school at Notre Dame showed up and saw me spend most of the game on the bench.

Coach Yeagley basically viewed that Notre Dame game as having our asses handed to us by a much lesser team, and he was angry enough to spit flames. With the bus idling in the Notre Dame parking lot, relatives and friends milling around it, he stood at the front of the aisle and unloaded on us.

"Let me make something really clear right up front, guys," he said. "Whatever it was you were doing out there was not Indiana soccer. Not even close."

He paused, looked around the bus, and then we felt the blast furnace heat of his frustration.

"What the hell was going through your heads out there?" he shouted. "You played almost an entire game and an overtime with your heads up your asses. How does that happen?"

He stopped again, shaking his head.

"Well, here's what's next: There are going to be some changes around here and I mean *immediately*." He gave that last word extra volume. "Tomorrow. Everybody better come to practice with their heads someplace other than where they were today because every spot on this team is up for grabs. Every single spot."

Coach was letting everything fly, dropping f-bombs here and there. I'd never heard him yell like that before. I had never seen him so upset and dismayed with the direction and potential future of this program. The bus door was closed, as were the tinted windows.

I looked at the suddenly very quiet cluster of players' families and friends and wondered if they were hearing what was going on inside.

"We are going to find the right formula for bringing IU soccer back and some of you aren't going to be very happy about it and that'll be too bad. I've seen enough of this horseshit."

He must have felt we'd picked up right where we'd left off from last year and were heading deeper into the black hole. I have to say, we deserved every bit of his wrath. We played flat, and the mood of the whole program was sort of aimless, drifting. It felt like we didn't know who we were or where we'd come from, what it meant to be an IU soccer team. And, part of me thought Coach Yeagley was struggling, too, on the inside. I wondered whether he still was having second thoughts about cutting loose those players last year and whether the concerns of what those moves would mean long-term for the program were pressing harder on him or whether word would circulate that Yeagley was too much of an old-school hard guy who couldn't deal with today's elite players. He was in a tough place. I felt bad for him.

The bus ride home, normally a pretty fun time filled with music, goofing around and laughter, was silent. All I heard was the drone and groan of the bus for almost four hours. Everybody stared out the window or slept. And you could feel a little anxiety, a little fear spreading throughout the team.

We had some soul-searching to do in the next few days. On Monday, we went back to the grind, and things seemed to intensify a bit. We tried to forget about Notre Dame and just focus on playing high-energy, fundamentally tough soccer. I could see Coach Yeagley trying some new combinations of players. He stayed true to his rant about all of us fighting for positions, that nothing was set in stone, and that anyone could be playing at any time. It instilled some internal competition and elevated the overall play of each man on the roster, just what the coaches wanted, I guess. And, it played right into my strengths. Scrapping for recognition was something I'd become accustomed to doing every single day over the last four years and couple months.

The next game was at home against Memphis State, and Coach Yeagley indeed did mix up the lineup a bit, inserting sophomores Kenny Godat, a midfielder, and Jim Crockford, a center back, as starters. Coach switched goalkeepers as well, replacing Bruce Killough with Juergen Sommer, a very confident freshman walk-on who stood about 6-feet-4-inches and had worked extremely hard in practice to earn the back-up role. And then coach inserted a fourth new starter: me, at outside midfielder. This time there was no cheering or slaps on the back. Mine was just another name in the lineup and, unlike the last time, I was completely ready to do what I do. No nerves about losing my position. No doubts about whether I belong. Running through my system was a strange mix of calm and crackling energy. I was captain. I had a responsibility, and I was going to hit it head on. I may not ever have been as focused and centered as I was when we walked up the hill to Armstrong Stadium.

Now I'm smart enough to know that what happened over the next few weeks had a little to do with my skills and more to do with my heart and that what happened over the next few weeks was a team effort in every sense of the phrase. But I also know this: I was a part of what happened over the next few weeks, a starter on that team—a captain—and what happened was what some people might call incredible.

We started by beating Memphis State 3-1. Afterward, Coach Yeagley was really pumped.

"That's what we're looking for, boys," he said. I could see that he was pretty sure he'd found the right lineup moves and that gave him enormous satisfaction. He had a little of the old confidence back. "Loved the effort, guys. Let's keep after it."

Two days later, we clobbered Ohio State 5-0, and the beautiful thing about that game was that each goal was scored by a different guy, including the first-ever goal by senior John Trask, who went on to be an assistant coach at IU and head coach at University of Wisconsin. Talk about a team effort, eh? That game also was the first shutout for Juergen, who went on to play in the World Cup and professionally in the U.S. and Europe for several years.

We went to Bowling Green a couple of days after that and beat them 3-1. That's when freshman Kenny Snow started to assert his staggering ability to score, firing two in the back of the net, making for seven goals in seven games. The week after that, Akron, always a tough opponent for us, came to Bloomington. They were ranked No. 4, and we beat them 1-0, on a goal by guess who? Big-timer Pete Stoyanovich.

We went to St. Louis in late September to play another really gritty opponent, St. Louis University, in a game that took on added importance because we had five guys on our roster from the St. Louis area. This would be a serious test for what had become our four-game winning streak, and it started poorly. The Billikens scored first, less than two minutes into the game, which made for a very unsettling start for an inexperienced team like ours.

It was the last time St. Louis would score. Led by two goals from Kenny Snow and another by freshman Chris Sciortino, the first of his career—he happened to be from St. Louis—we beat the Billikens 3-1. What I remember about that game was that St. Louis was pissed after we took control, and they started to play a really rugged style designed to beat up an opponent and break them down psychologically. It can be very effective, especially against a team with a lot of newcomers, like ours. Except it wasn't.

With about three minutes left, the game was pretty much over. We had a throw-in, and I was standing, facing my teammate, Dave Eise, on the sideline. Dave threw the ball in to me. I didn't know it, but a St. Louis player standing a few yards away had been sizing me up and took off running as the ball was in the air. He cleaned me out at the ankles from behind, and I hit the ground hard. It was a vindictive, petty move that could have seriously injured me.

But it didn't. With trainer John Schrader at my side, my head cleared and I stood up. The first thought that occurred to me was hockey—a very popular sport in St. Louis—and the name that came to my mind was Al Secord, known as somewhat of a goon enforcer when he was with the Chicago Blackhawks, my favorite hockey team.

I shook the cobwebs and shouted, "Holy cow, I think Secord just hit me."

The guys liked that one—especially Stoyo, who I sort of directed it to—and they erupted in laughter, which was sweet music to my ears, almost as sweet as the victory. St. Louis' players were less amused, and that was okay, too. The message was sent: The Billikens had thrown everything they could at us. We took the punches and just steamrolled through them. Now we're laughing. This was a team that was having a lot of fun together, a team that was pulling itself into one very strong unit.

In the sports vernacular, IU was on a roll. We appeared in the rankings for the first time, cracking the top 20. We welcomed Miami of Ohio to Bloomington but were unkind hosts, walloping the Redskins, the school's nickname back then, 8-0 in a game that had great personal significance. While the score was still relatively close, Stoyo took a shot from outside and the rebound ricocheted to the front. Years of being focused on those rebounds came into play. I was charging like I always did but got ensnared in a cluster of Miami defenders. I managed to fight through them inside the 6-yard box and punched a loose ball with my left foot. It ran between the legs of a defender past the goalkeeper to the back of the net. After more than four years, I'd scored my first collegiate goal!

It may not have made ESPN's highlight videos. You could even call it a "garbage goal." But you'd never have thought so judging by the wild celebration that erupted from my teammates, who all knew it was my first one. I was more excited than any man has a right to be. Fifteen minutes later, Stoyo took a direct kick from about 20 yards away. The ball rebounded off the crossbar to me—I loved when Stoyo was thoughtful like that—as the goalkeeper lunged left. I gathered the rebound and slid the ball just inside the far post. Suddenly, I was a scoring machine!

Just as suddenly, we moved up the rankings to number 8 in the nation and headed to a tournament in Evansville, the Kenny Kent Classic, where we played a scrappy and previously unbeaten Seton Hall, who was ranked number 7 in the nation. They clawed and scratched and muscled us into overtime, and we won 3-2 on goals by Kenny Snow and Han Roest. The next day we had a much easier time with Wake Forest, beating the Demon Deacons 4-0 and claiming the championship trophy.

In early October, it was Northwestern's turn. We torched them 7-0 and moved up to number 3 in the rankings. I could hear "Back in the High Life Again" ringing in my ears everywhere I walked. I'm pretty sure the whole team could.

Marquette came to town, and we beat them by the same score we beat Northwestern, 7-0. Kenny Snow was scoring goals on a head-spinning pace. He had 20 entering that game, and we'd won 10 in a row.

On October 16, we went to Cleveland to play Cleveland State, and they scored twice against us. But we scored six times against them. Two days later, Southern Illinois University-Edwardsville, soccer giant killers, played us at home, and we beat them, too, by a 3-0 score. That made it 12 in a row.

October was drawing to a close, and Evansville University, another stout, in-state rival that always gave us fits, came to Armstrong Stadium. They stuck it to us good; they dug in and played some of the toughest defense we saw all year, and we beat them, 1-0. Thirteen in a row.

Practices were loose. The coaches were upbeat. "Casanova," by Levert was blaring in the locker room, along with "Back in the High Life Again," of course. We genuinely liked each other, and we had achieved that rare balance of intensity and fun that made for the all-important and often elusive chemistry, something Indianapolis Star reporter Jim Uebelhoer sensed.

"Camaraderie—which was painfully absent the past two years—is the main reason the Hoosiers are opening some eyes again this season," he wrote in an October piece in the *Star*. Then he quoted Coach Yeagley, who also appeared to notice.

"This team works very hard for each other," coach told Uebelhoer. "They put forth the effort to make each other look good. They enjoy playing together."

I stayed very focused on team chemistry. It seemed so instinctive to me that any team endeavor needs a robust, genuine dose of it to be really successful. I sort of improvised a recipe centered around a few basics. One of the main ingredients was making everybody a part of this ride, regardless of their contributions. That's how guys like Pat McGauley, Stolly, Keith, and Mickey McCartney made me feel back when I was little more than a dust ball on the floor. So everybody moved goals and shagged soccer balls.

I also made it a point to talk to everybody—coaches, trainers, brightest stars on our team, and the lowliest 34th man—all the time. In the locker room, training room, on the practice field, everywhere, I was talking. I greeted everybody as they walked in the locker room and said goodbye to each one as they left, every day. Talking probably was my most prominent trait. On the field, whether it was practices or games, I constantly was talking— not trash talking, though. I was into the exact opposite; always encouraging, affirming, and communicating everything that was unfolding in front of us. Even if I was on somebody, the criticism was constructive, telling the guy he could do it and always trying to inject humor, the great stress reliever and cohesive force. We were working hard in practice, cranking up the tunes and dancing in the locker room, laughing at my stretches, and having a lot of fun off the field as well. Despite all that, we kept intact our reputations around campus as a hard-working group of guys who followed the rules.

I wanted to create and perpetuate that positive energy every single day, and it looked like it was working, so I stayed with it.

We had truly developed a family atmosphere, and it extended beyond the coaches and players on the roster. My parents and Sherri were on cloud nine coming to every game and staying after to take groups of us to dinner. Mom and dad were having so much fun they'd end up driving back to Indianapolis after some games as late as midnight. In every one of our conversations, mom wanted to hear every twist and turn of the season. It seemed like her mantra was, "I want to hear all of the details. Start from the beginning." As I told it, she'd pepper me with questions throughout my explanation. My parents loved the team, and the players loved my parents. My brothers Danny and Pete came to a bunch of games, as did my sister Deanne. Even my youngest brother, Dino, busy with his own stellar high school soccer career, made it to a few. We were writing letters back and forth. I was having the most fun of my life. It felt like a bus rolling along the Electric Happy Highway. It got pretty crowded, and I loved everybody on board and every mile of the ride. It was as good as it gets.

One of the greatest things about all this was Sherri's presence. She was there the whole time. Sherri and her roommates became our biggest fans. She'd attend every home game and was there waiting for me when we'd return from the road. After each match, we'd talk about it for a little while, allowing me to decompress, and then talk about us and other things. She was no soccer expert, which made it more fun for me, and her upbeat support and stability were incredible. Our practice of attending church together in the summer continued through the fall and anchored me through what could have been a disorienting odyssey. My life had such balance. I couldn't believe how lucky I was.

On Halloween, the team boarded a flight and headed to California to play in the UCLA-MetLife Classic. We were pretty excited about the trip out west for a few reasons. It was cool to represent Indiana University soccer on a west coast trip. It's just not something that happens too often in a college soccer player's career. Plus, it was the longest trip of the year for us, which meant we would spend time together as a team. And, for this team, a group that genuinely enjoyed being together, it was going to be a terrific chance to pull together even closer, have a few laughs, and make memories that would last a lifetime. The vibe definitely was electric and upbeat.

On top of all that, it was a real challenge for us to play against these two ranked, west coast programs. Teams out there traditionally are stacked with excellent talent and flashy players, a pretty distinct contrast to the Midwestern, grind-it-out style we played. The tournament would go a long way toward showing just how much we belonged with the big dogs. It was a significant test and I think every last one of us very clearly understood that.

Our first game was against San Diego State, a national powerhouse that would end up going deep into the NCAA post-season championship tournament that year. It was a great game, but not for the reasons you might think. To compound the pressure on us that weekend, it rained steadily and, at times, really hard in Los Angeles, making the fields extremely sloppy. Pockets of standing water were interspersed with soggy turf and mud. And, we did not play our best game. It was the soccer equivalent of the baseball scenario in which a pitcher takes the mound without his best stuff but digs deep and tries to find a way to get the job done. That's what we did against the Aztecs. We found a way to win, 3-2, and advanced to the championship against UCLA on their home field on Sunday afternoon.

Road trips can really solidify teams and promote unity, and, just like we had hoped before boarding the plane to the west coast, that's exactly what happened on this trip. We had some free time on Saturday and, even though the rain wouldn't stop, tried to take advantage of what was supposed to be sunny Southern California. We got out and walked the streets of L.A., ate at a restaurant, and cruised some stores. We even visited one of those individual recording studios that started sprouting around the country then. It's like recording your karaoke experience. You walk in the studio, pick a song, pay your fee, strap on the headphones, and step up to the microphone. The studio plays the music, supplies you with lyrics, and you sing with everything you have. Afterward, the nice people there hand you a tape of your masterpiece. Some of us sang solo; some went in as groups. It was a riot. Dave Eise and I sang "Tender Love," by Force MDs, and you know, we weren't too bad. Still waiting for our recording contract.

Those down times were the icing on the cake in terms of camaraderie. Turns out we needed all of the togetherness we could muster. Much more than San Diego State, the UCLA Bruins were a perennial powerhouse. They had a rich tradition, a great coach, several All-Americans on the roster, and played a beautiful style of soccer. They also hadn't lost at home in something like 30 or 40 games.

Sherri's brother Kurt, an IU grad who was living in L.A. at the time, came to watch the game, and it was great seeing a friendly face on the road. It gave me an extra spark, not that I needed one. We took a hard-nosed, toe-to-toe approach with them in what may have been muddiest field I've ever played on, created from two consecutive days of rain. The conditions were physically exhausting and produced a very rough game. Both sides racked up lots of fouls, especially in the second half. But I could see that we had the old IU approach, playing as if we knew we weren't going to lose, yet never taking anything for granted, hustling nonstop, and contesting everything. Team confidence combined with a hunger, both of which we had built throughout the season. And, that, friends, is a wonderful thing. Kenny Snow scored twice, and the final score was IU 2, UCLA 1.

Those two games were near-epic wins for us. Two road victories against premier, west coast teams. We were flying before we boarded the plane. On top of everything else, I made the All-Tournament team that weekend, an honor typically awarded to All-Americans and players with much higher pedigree than mongrel Whitey Kapsalis. Back home was just as crazy for a different but related reason. My brother Dino's high school team won the Indiana state championship the same weekend.

In L.A., we celebrated our tourney championship briefly then headed to the airport and took a red-eye flight back home to Bloomington. When I opened the door to my apartment, I could barely hold up my head I was so tired. And then my eye caught something on the kitchen table—a balloon floating above flowers and a giant chocolate chip cookie. "Congratulations, Whitey!" the icing on the cookie proclaimed. "Love, Sherri." I just couldn't believe this was happening to me. As tired as I was, I had to eat that cookie, and it was the sweetest treat I've ever had. Two years earlier, Sherri barely knew me or anything about the sport. Now, it was pretty clear that our relationship was deep, abiding, and growing. It also was pretty clear that everyone close to me was becoming a fan of IU soccer. I loved it all.

We had one game left in the regular season at Wisconsin, another team that always fought us every second of the game. Seemed like contests against the Badgers, win or lose, were decided by one goal and often in overtime. They were unranked this year but, especially in their old fortress of a stadium, a very formidable opponent. Fan turnout was small compared to what we got at IU, but in keeping with the Badger faithful, it always was as hostile as any crowd we faced. They really loved to beat IU. All that made Madison among the most difficult places to play. And, on this particular November day—Madison is almost 400 miles north of Bloomington—the air was really frosty. We had to fight through an evenly matched game, clamping down on defense. When time ran out, we'd won, 2-0. Sixteen consecutive wins, a record-tying accomplishment for IU soccer. Our ranking: Numero uno. If I hadn't have lived it, I would have thought it impossible.

The celebration in the locker room and the bus was wild. We were hooting it up, singing along with "Back in the High Life Again," and laughing, laughing a lot. Everybody was wide-eyed with excitement at what we'd done. Maybe it was just sinking in, and the beauty of it was that we had a seven-hour bus ride to let it sink in. It was the greatest bus trip of my life. By winning at Wisconsin and securing the nation's number 1 ranking, we earned a bye in the first round of the NCAA tournament. More importantly, we had grown so much as a team, as a group of guys, as a family. We really loved each other.

By the time the regular season was over, we had put together a phenomenal ride; unthinkable when you consider where we'd started in August. And, personally, I'd proven that I belonged, scoring six goals that year, good enough for third highest on the team.

We had role players. We had versatile stars. We had the song in our ears. We had the chemistry, genuinely caring about each other and playing hard-nosed, enthusiastic soccer for each other. We had all of it and then some. In the end, we just won. We found whatever it took inside us and just won, baby.

Going into the NCAA tournament in mid-November, IU, the team that was unranked and in disarray in August, was the best college team in the country. Back in the high life. And the kid who was never going to play there was its captain.

How about that for a dream come true?

Wearing the IU jersey and being alongside my teammates in the starting line-up was an incredible feeling....
one that I will always cherish.

8

Life is beautiful when everything comes together.

THE UNEXPECTED BEAUTY OF DREAMS

CHAPTER 8:

THE UNEXPECTED
BEAUTY OF DREAMS

Four post-season games stood between us and the national championship—a ludicrous thought at the start of the season— and our No. 1 ranking earned us a break in the first week of the tournament. While every other team played, we got a much-deserved rest and practiced.

Our first opponent was Clemson, and I have to admit when I heard that, a little anxiety flared in me. The Tigers were our nemesis. Remember, they beat IU in the 1984 national championship game, beat us the year after that at our place in the prominent Classic and embarrassed us in 1986 in a late-season game that pretty much killed our post-season tournament chances.

This year, Clemson was particularly dangerous. They squeaked in the tournament as a 24th seed and, playing like the loose, all-out underdogs that they were, won their first game. With that victory, they'd officially gone farther than anyone had expected. Every game after that was icing, another fun ride on their amusement-park season. Suddenly, I was nervous and regretful about our one-week rest. I wondered if it stalled our momentum.

I also felt a little unsteady in part because this was my first, real playoff experience at IU. The three other times we'd made the tournament, the closest I'd come was practicing with the team. I hadn't even suited up. That inexperience was something the entire team shared. This year's roster included 12 freshmen—the most since IU started its program in 1973—and four red-shirts from the 1986 team.

But the game would be at our place and that gave me confidence and excitement. The crowd would be with us.

Game day arrived. It was late November, and the crisp fall had given way to the more serious bite of the coming winter. The sky was pewter colored. The last of the fall leaves in wooded, rolling Bloomington were fading. In a couple of days, we'd be on Thanksgiving break.

When we jogged on the field for warm-ups, more than 4,000 people in Armstrong Stadium cheered. We might have been overwhelmed by it all. I know I was feeling a little extra pressure, different from the typical, pre-game jitters that flash in my stomach and chest. It might have had something to do with my awareness that I was a little foggy from the week off and my sensitivity to Clemson's history against us. Maybe we were all thinking the same thing: *This Clemson team is really dangerous. We need to put this game out of reach early and start our unstoppable roll to the championship.*

From the opening kick, instead of displaying that ferocious confidence, we were a little manic. We did come out with a lot of energy, firing shot after shot, but Clemson withstood every push we made. Then Sean Shapert, a critical guy for us who had a school record 18 assists that season, took a knee to his back on what looked an awful lot like a flagrant foul, although none was called. He played a few more minutes in the first half, but just couldn't compete and sat the rest of the game.

Thank God for Stoyo. Ever the big game player, he stepped up again. Late in the first half, he managed to streak behind the defense, gather a ball from Kenny Snow and fire a shot from the right an instant before the Clemson goalkeeper skidded into him. That spectacular score put us on top and lit a spark.

The second half was an entirely different game. After taking only three shots in the first half, the Tigers came out fired up and were winning balls all over the field. They took 13 shots and got two late goals.

With about five minutes remaining, Herb Haller fired a pass to Kenny Snow, but it was a couple feet too far ahead of him. Kenny, the national scoring leader, couldn't get his full force behind the ball but launched a valiant shot anyway. The Clemson goalkeeper was able to catch up to it. In 40 minutes of the second half, that was our only shot on goal. Clemson hung on. Final score: 2-1.

When time expired, the Clemson guys and the few Tiger fans who'd made the trip exploded, jumping for joy, pumping fists, and whooping it up on our field. They'd just beaten the number one team in the country.

It seemed to unfold in slow motion and felt like some surreal, out-of-body experience. Standing on the field, out of breath, sweat cooling all over my body, I was so wracked with pain and disbelief that I went numb. Everything inside me was still. Unwilling to process what was happening in plain sight, I couldn't cry, couldn't even seem to breathe. I think all of us were stunned silent and crushed. The Tigers had done it again. This was our fourth consecutive loss to them and the first post-season tournament game we'd lost at home in 19 contests.

I looked over to Stoyo, who was particularly upset. He sat on the bench, tears in his eyes while he took off his shoes and shin guards.

"Whitey," he said, "that's it. That's our last game together. I can't believe this is over. I just can't believe it's done."

I couldn't believe it, either. I approached and sat with him, looking over the field, watching the Clemson celebration. I still didn't cry. The numbness was holding on. How could this have happened? We were the best darn team in the nation. We'd proved it game after game after game, pouring everything we had into each one.

Looking back, I guess it was one of those contests you see premier teams deal with in the post-season from time to time. They run into a freewheeling, hard-charging underdog and have the sweat scared out of them but pull out a close victory then go on a run all the way to the championship. Or, the underdog squeaks out a shocker. We'd just been shocked. The storybook, national championship dream had exploded in front of our eyes. We were finished.

We made our way to the locker room and changed in silence and tears. It was especially tough on the guys, like me, who weren't coming back. Coach Yeagley entered a few minutes later and clearly was upset, heartbroken, not so much because of our performance but because of how much he liked this team.

"This has been one of my proudest, most rewarding seasons," he told us at one point, and he got a little choked up. "And I'm disappointed, but I've never enjoyed a year as much as I've enjoyed this one with you guys."

He meant it. Coach Yeagley always was careful to avoid comparing one team too closely to another, but you could see how much he loved us for what we'd done to bring the program back from the ruins. He'd made some tough, risky decisions, and we made those decisions look very wise. I know he appreciated that.

We shed more tears but left them in the locker room. A bunch of us went to dinner at Macri's Deli, rehashing game moments, doing the old woulda-coulda-shoulda. It was our own group therapy session. None of us wanted to go home and just stare at the walls — or punch holes in them. Together at least we could process the misery. By the time everybody separated around midnight, I was still somber but feeling a little better. Through all the tears and hugs, I think I began to appreciate what an unforgettable journey we'd travelled.

The next day, I woke up and dragged myself, zombie-like, through my classes. Maybe that was helpful, too. Better to keep busy than to sit around feeling sorry for myself. But that day was particularly challenging. In the afternoon, we trudged over to the locker room and, instead of practicing for our next opponent on the road to the national championship, we cleared lockers and turned in our gear. It was our final team meeting of the year — my last team meeting forever.

I was pulling stuff from my stall when teammate John Trask walked over to me.

"Hey Whitey, let me see your practice ball," he said.

I reached in the locker, grabbed the scuffed, battered thing and held it in front of him.

Without a word, he took it from my hands, pulled out a black marker and signed it, then passed it to the next guy, who signed and passed it. In a couple minutes, all 15-20 guys in the locker room had signed it.

In five years of being in that room, I'd never seen anybody sign anybody else's soccer ball. I don't know exactly how to express what it felt like. Looking back, all of what had happened over the past few months seems almost magical; one experience after another so amazing, so joyous, so heartbreaking, so filled with emotion. But this one was really powerful, I think, because it was spontaneous and happened in a place that was central and intimate to my journey. Whatever the case, I was caught completely off-guard and couldn't hold back the tears. I had so much love for the guys in that room. We all had it for each other, and that, everyone knows, is extremely rare.

Coach Yeagley came in and called us together.

He kept his comments brief, reiterated what he'd told us in the locker room the day before, and gave out the final two team awards of the season. Kenny Snow won Most Valuable Player, and I won the Mental Attitude Award. Two years in a row. Pretty cool. The guys were generous with their cheers. They clapped, slapped both of us on the backs, gave us high fives. Before he left, Coach Yeagley signed the ball, too.

All of that helped ease the gloom a little but it still hung over the whole team, me in particular, for a few days. Then we scattered home for Thanksgiving break, which probably was a healthy thing. Clemson ended up winning the national championship in their home stadium a couple weeks later. A record crowd of more than 8,300 watched them beat San Diego State 2-0, the same team we'd beaten toward the end of the regular season.

I returned to campus and was a regular college student for a few weeks, something I really didn't enjoy. Soccer had consumed such a huge wedge of my life that when it ended, this wide, empty expanse opened in front of me like some flat desert. I was a little lost without soccer. Maybe more than a little. As grueling as practice was, I missed it, and of course I missed the excitement of games, the experience of being around a team focused on a common objective, the camaraderie of the locker room, the bus rides, and looking forward to the next match. I missed all of it.

I graduated in December, moved back home to Carmel, lived with my parents, and went to work for the family's soccer retail business. We opened a second store in Indianapolis, and I managed the place. My relationship with Sherri continued to grow. She was set to graduate in May the following year, which meant I ended up spending a lot of time in Bloomington, traveling there almost every weekend partly to see her, partly to cling to something I knew I'd never experience again, and partly to hang out with Stoyo.

The Clemson loss did turn out to be his last soccer game. After that, Stoyo focused on football full-time, and the team had some serious success, making consecutive trips to the Peach Bowl and Liberty Bowl. I went to almost all of IU's home games to see my guy rip the ball through the uprights and deep downfield on kickoffs. His incredible focus and work ethic were paying off. Stoyo was second team All-American his junior year. By the time he finished his final season, he'd become IU's record holder for field goals in a season, extra points in a season, and consecutive points. NFL teams' interest in him heightened, and it was really exciting for me to observe it all gather momentum.

After IU's football team won the 1988 Liberty Bowl, Stoyo ramped up his efforts even more. The NFL Scouting Combines—a grueling four days of drills for hundreds of college football players with professional aspirations—were slated for February in Indianapolis. To prepare, Stoyo wanted to kick and kick and kick. I became his practice holder. We'd grab his ginormous boom box, head over to the IU field house, and blast tunes while he tore balls out of my hand into a net. Stoyo loved his Bananarama, especially "Cruel Summer." I remember how happy he was then, how happy I was for him, seeing that he'd come through the loss of his mother and had such exciting prospects for the future.

Stoyo turned out to be pretty happy at the combines, too, where he nailed 35 of his 35 field goal attempts. Scouts noticed. A few weeks later, the Miami Dolphins came calling, drafting Stoyo in the eighth round.

IU's soccer team looked like it was picking up where we'd left off a year earlier. I attended every home game, went to practices once in a while, and kept in touch with Coach Yeagley and a couple players. The guys were as tough as we had been the year before, tougher maybe after going through that last season and forging a strong team bond. "The pieces were in place," the IU year-by-year history recap states about the 1988 season. "The only question was if the squad would be able to put them together."

Much like my first couple of years on the team, I'd cheer them on from the stands and hang out at their apartments after games, games that usually ended in victory. Led by Kenny Snow, Sean Shapert, and Juergen Sommer, the Hoosiers won 9 of their first 10 games, then lost a pair, won 6 of the next 7, and entered the NCAA post-season tournament ranked ninth in the nation. That must have been a more comfortable spot than the number one we'd had going into the tournament a year earlier because the Hoosiers rolled through the post season, beating Boston University, Seton Hall, and Portland.

That brought them to the championship against Howard at IU's Armstrong Stadium. A group of us—Sherri, Stolly, Stoyo, Keith, Pat McGauley, Mickey McCartney, me, and a few others—tailgated in the parking lot before the game. Then we crowded into the stands with nearly 5,200 other fans and cheered so long and loud that our voices became hoarse. It was worth it. Sean Shapert, who'd gotten injured in our season-ending loss to Clemson a year earlier, scored on a penalty kick. IU won, 1-0. The Hoosiers had returned to the mountain top, best in the land, national champions.

When time expired, our group jumped and hooted and hugged, overwhelmed with joy. We ran down and watched the guys celebrate by hoisting the trophy as they jogged around the track that surrounded the field. For a second or two, I thought about what might have been and almost drifted into an alternative vision of what I was seeing on the field; an alternative vision that included Stoyo, me, and last years' team enjoying a similar on-field championship celebration. But that wasn't reality, and that was just fine. I was over-the-top excited for these guys on this team. That's all I had room for in my heart.

A couple weeks after the championship, I came home from work and found an envelope on the kitchen table addressed to me. Inside was an invitation to the soccer team's championship banquet. I was surprised and a little confused. It's a relatively intimate affair that alums are never invited to; only players, their families, a few university people, and big supporters of the soccer program get to attend. I figured Coach Yeagley must have come up with a new policy of inviting a bunch of alums back to the banquet. *That was cool,* I thought, and I started looking forward to getting caught up with the guys, hearing details about the post-season run, and celebrating one more time.

Dressed in a suit and tie, I walked into the university union with Sherri on a frosty night. The ballroom sparkled. Eight or so circular tables were draped in white linen. All the guys greeted me warmly. I looked around for other alums but didn't see any. After hearing anecdotes of the championship season in clusters of four or five people, I spotted Bruce Killough and we chatted for a few moments. Among the 70 or so people attending, we were the only soccer alums.

After a while, we all sat down to a delicious chicken dinner—championship chicken, which is always delicious. It could have been cold, greasy nuggets from a paper box and I would have savored it, with or without sauce. That year's co-captain, Herb Haller, started the speeches. Standing at the microphone, he talked about the wonderful season, hit on a few high points, and said how fulfilling it was to bring IU back to the top, how players were there for each other the entire season, and how so many people contributed and supported the team.

Then Herb paused and looked at me.

"The only regret I have," Herb said, "is that the guys who had the most to do with this championship run—Whitey and Bruce—weren't on the team."

People started cheering. I sat there, stunned, trying to suppress the humility, gratitude, and overwhelming emotion flowing through me.

Next was assistant coach Joe Kelly, who said the same thing, only elaborated, saying it was a shame Bruce and I didn't get championship rings. People broke into applause again. Then came assistant coach Don Rawson.

"I know it's been said," Coach Rawson said, "I just want to reiterate what an impact these guys had on this program."

Wow. I glanced at Bruce, a guy I really admired, and I was just as excited for him as I was for me. Even though Bruce had become a back-up goalkeeper early in our final season and was a lot more reserved than I, he'd remained a leader off the field and, more important, never let his personal agenda and disappointment at being a nonstarter detract from that leadership or the team's overall best interests. His off-the-field contributions were crucial.

Then it was Coach Yeagley's turn. He said the same about me and Bruce as the others had. I found out that coach already had put his sentiments to paper, sending my parents a letter months earlier saying I was "one of the finest leaders I have been fortunate enough to be associated with over the years." He even sent them a Christmas card. "Paul was the greatest!" he wrote. "He's a winner in all respects!"

I swallowed. I couldn't believe what I was hearing, especially from Coach Yeagley, who'd been my biggest doubter and harshest critic. I've gone over those moments many times in my mind and still can't identify exactly what I did. I'm sure I was beaming, and I recall feeling my eyes well up. A part of me wanted to shout for joy and let out all that emotion in an explosion of tears. But that would be really bad form. This was the team's night, not mine. I remembered what my parents taught us about being humble and did all I could to hold in what I was feeling. It was pretty uncomfortable, but in an ecstatic way, if that makes sense. I'd been so grateful just to get invited. Then this happened. Me, a guy who was pegged as a nobody, sat there taking in all that genuine, spontaneous gratitude for a championship season in which I never competed. The what-if question? Answered. That dream I'd been chasing? I guess I'd finally caught it.

After the speeches, we stood, said our goodbyes and slowly made our way into the cold night. I told many of the guys who said those kind things about me how much I appreciated their remarks and congratulated them again. But they just kept thanking me.

They never did see me cry. That I saved for the drive back home.

While I rolled up Highway 37, I thought how different that night's trip was from the first trip I'd taken to IU to meet Coach Yeagley in the lobby of Assembly Hall. I thought about all that I'd experienced on a five-year odyssey. I'd gone from fighting just to get and hang on to the very bottom spot on a soccer team—a guy with no chance of playing who in fact was encouraged to leave, whose career nearly ended because of an injury—to becoming the captain and two-time mental attitude award winner of the number one team in the country. I found myself wondering what would have happened if I hadn't roomed with Stolly and Keith, if I'd transferred to University of Southern Indiana, if my little champ of a fifth metatarsal had failed me, if I hadn't become close friends with Stoyo, if I hadn't met Sherri, or if Coach Yeagley had never given me a chance, never made me captain. I thought about how I'd grown and changed in ways I never could have predicted and became someone I had no idea existed, a leader. All I'd wanted was to play soccer.

If someone had told me how difficult it was going to be, I probably would have taken the easy road out, but that's the beauty of naiveté, right? And, the beauty of dreams. We don't know what's ahead of us. We don't always get to a place we may have anticipated or get there the way we figured we would. But we must not give in to doubt or fear. If we've got passion for the things we believe in and we're willing to work hard, it all becomes worth it in ways we couldn't have imagined.

Last year, I heard a fascinating talk by Lisa Bu, a manager for TED, the widely known nonprofit speakers forum that, as it says, is "devoted to ideas worth spreading." Of the many intriguing insights she shared in an incredibly full six minutes, I found one particularly powerful.

"I have come to believe," Lisa said, "that coming true is not the only purpose of a dream. It's most important purpose is to get us in touch with where dreams come from, where passion comes from, where happiness comes from. Even a shattered dream can do that for you."

I thoroughly enjoyed my journey, and I think many people can see why. It ended pretty spectacularly. But that dream also was very fragile and highly tenuous at times. For those whose dreams don't end the way mine did, well, I hope you found where dreams come from, where passion comes from, and where happiness comes from. If you haven't, take another look at that dream and your journey toward it. You might be surprised. See, I really believe that there is no such thing as failure. A dream vigorously pursued is a success, no matter the outcome.

As uncomfortable as this is for me to say, I'm proud of what I accomplished. But this journey was really about much more than me. Sure, I had to overcome obstacles and yeah, I learned invaluable lessons about discipline, team structure, pushing myself, and about leadership and the commitment to winning. They are lessons that set the tone of my personal and professional life and will stay with me for the rest of my life. I'm eternally grateful for that.

But I hope my story can inspire others to believe in themselves, set goals, be persistent, persevere, and surround themselves with quality, supportive people. Whatever your age, whatever dream you choose, keep after it. Dream big.

I find another aspect of the journey just as fascinating, maybe even more so. This odyssey really was about this thing we had built, and it makes me think that team sports—even life—is not so much about personal accomplishments to advance self, but more about personal accomplishments to advance the team or even society. If you take one thing away from my story, I hope it's this: that my journey redefines winning as being more about everyone's personal growth and less about a won-loss record and more about inspiring others and less about an individual accomplishment. That's where true fulfillment is. "Winning" in the conventional sense is a by-product of that approach. It's how authentic champions are made and legacies built, at least that's how I view it. I hope my story inspires you to move in that team-advancing direction, even just a little, on your personal journey.

* * *

IU soccer went on to win five more national championships for a total of eight, as of this writing, and I'm pretty sure the guys will bring home more championship trophies to crowd the display case at Assembly Hall. Coach Yeagley, who I still stay in touch with, retired in 2003 after coaching for 31 years at IU and winning six of those national championships. The coach at the helm for the latest championship in 2012 was a young up-and-coming guy named Todd Yeagley, Jerry's son. Gotta love that IU soccer legacy, huh?

I still stay in touch with Stoyo, Stolly, Keith, Mickey McCartney, Pat McGauley, and John Johnson. In fact, those teammates remain my closest friends decades after we played for the cream and crimson. When I get down to Bloomington two or three times a year, usually for soccer games, I run into other teammates, and the memories and emotions come rushing back. The connection we have is extraordinary, something I truly marvel at and cherish.

I framed my number 14 jersey, and it hangs in my office, where I look at it every day. That battered soccer ball from my final IU team meeting is deflated now and a little dusty. The signatures have faded. But I've hung onto it and have kept it tucked away in my den. Once in a while, I sneak down there alone, dig it out, brush it off, and remember.

I've stepped away from soccer except for coaching kids' programs, including my own kids' teams. I love working with them, love working with all kids.

And, I always encourage their dreams. I understand how those work.

Trey, Katrina and Nicolette provide purpose and blessings every day.

EPILOGUE: DREAM IT FORWARD

My college soccer experience was remarkable. All those events I've just finished telling you about have only grown in meaning over the years. And, like many adults, I've also learned a thing or two slogging through everyday life for a few decades. Throughout that time, working in sales, working with a lot of teams, and coaching kids and adults, I've used those lessons from my athletic days and beyond and synthesized them in ways I hope might be useful to others. Here you'll find my six principles, a few thoughts that seem to work in chasing dreams and, if you're lucky, catching them. Try these for yourself as starters, then build your own approach. They might inspire you, or you might use them to inspire someone to dream and help them get there. It only takes one person.

1. Set attainable goals. Decide where you want to be. Make that objective reachable, but also make it a real stretch. Write down your goals and why you want to get there. Place this list of goals in a spot where you'll see it every morning and every night. You might even want to compose a collage of photos and phrases from magazines that depict that objective or inspire you to go for it—some people call it a vision board—and place the collage alongside your goal document. When your head hits the pillow, say a little affirmative prayer each night. Don't worry about how or when you're going to get there. That's for much higher powers to figure out. Once you've established your goals, commit yourself to hard work, patience, honesty, integrity, and consistency in reaching them. Be positive and kind. Don't deflate others in your own desire to succeed. In fact, encourage others. More on that later. When you reach that goal, set another goal and begin the process all over again.

2. Have dreams. This is the pie-in-the-sky, seemingly unreachable, fantasy stuff. President of the United States, your own tropical island, hitting a home run in the World Series, playing lead guitar in front of thousands, sailing around the world, winning the Nobel Peace Prize or an Academy Award, or designing a revolutionary sky scraper. Picture yourself in that position of achieving the dream. These dreams should not be an unhealthy obsession. They should be joyful and fun challenges that you embrace. I believe in planting seeds, surrendering, and then paying attention to indicators that your dream may be starting to come to fruition. In some ways, accomplishing dreams is out of our control, but planting a seed is well within our control. Plant the dream seed and then let it go. Like any seed, be sure to nourish it every once in a while, but don't stand over it to watch it grow. Dreams may take a while. Stay true to your goals and keep an eye on your dreams just often enough to keep them alive.

3. Surround yourself with supportive, enthusiastic, can-do people, and be one of those people. Relationships might be the most important piece of all. I was so fortunate to have been surrounded by people who believed in me, who allowed me to dream, and, in some cases, helped keep my dream alive. Be true to your relationships, be a good friend, be a good listener, and, sometimes, be a good cheerleader. Bring positive energy to relationships and seek out those who bring positive energy to you. What I found in pursuit of my dream was that the more supportive I was of others, the more support I received in return. Stay committed to being an enthusiastic, supportive, can-do person and other, like-minded people will be drawn to you. That churns the optimistic energy. Live out loud with positive energy and it comes back to you, and that is a thing of beauty.

4. Believe in yourself. I don't know what more to say about this one. It's related to all the others and yet stands alone; it needs to be stated and noted. You must know you can do whatever you set out to do. Your support system is critical, but in the end it is up to you. You define who you are. You define your goals and you define your dreams. Believing in yourself, balanced with a peaceful mind and incredible desire, is critical to achieving your dreams.

5. Persevere. Embrace the journey. Be willing to endure the rough patches—and those can be pretty rough and longer than you think—with the understanding that things may not go exactly as you had hoped and that you need to experience those difficulties to get where you want to go and that you will learn from these obstacles. Understand that dreams do come true, but not without challenges. Face the challenges head on and don't let them deter you from your desired outcome. Adversity reveals character: Do we plow ahead or give up? Do we make excuses or do we change to make things better? Do we take ownership or do we blame others? I have found that if you plow ahead, adapt to change as needed, and accept ownership, you give yourself a chance. Perseverance is not only the ability to overcome obstacles, but also the ability to stay with the plan long enough for it to unfold. Be patient and don't put timelines on dreams. Persevere and you'll come through everything a lot stronger and with more resolve. Also, no matter what, keep a healthy sense of humor. Learn to laugh at yourself and not take yourself so seriously. Believe me, life's a lot more fun that way.

6. Rely on your faith. Prayer is a very powerful thing. Let me repeat: Prayer is a very powerful thing. It is energy. It heals. It comforts. It gives courage. I lean on God throughout my day, every day, for the all-consuming concerns and smallest anxieties, for everything. It all starts and ends with Him. When you have done all that you can, relinquish control and rely on your faith. The sooner you place your full trust in Him and thank Him for all the abundance you have in your life, the sooner and more often you will walk through life with more prosperity, surer footing, a calmer mind, and loving heart. It's what I believe.

ACKNOWLEDGMENTS

To my Yia Yias and Papous, who started it all. My Mom and Dad, who molded, forged and built every fiber of my foundation—I am so grateful

Sherri, who deepens my faith daily and has been there through it all. Katrina, Nicolette and Trey who bring me love, joy, and purpose every day.

Pete, Dan, Deanne and Dean, who have provided unbridled enthusiasm and support my entire life. Nancy, Mike and Traci for their friendship and encouragement. All my aunts and uncles, cousins, nephews and nieces, and in-laws, who I love so much.

Coach Yeagley and his staff, who gave me a chance and guided the journey. My teammates and all alumni, specifically Keith, Stolly, Mickey, Stoyo, and JJ, who helped make this dream come true. Bigs, from whom I draw inspiration on a daily basis.

Teddy, who brought the story to life and for a cherished relationship as a result of working together. Bob Woerner, who guided me through the process.

Mary Fuller, who hired me for my first-ever public speaking engagement. The NCAA for the opportunity to be a featured speaker.

William O'Neil, who planted the initial seed of the project with his genuine interest. Kent Sterling, who never had a doubt.

Meyer and Meyer and Cardinal Publishing, for believing in the story.

Paul "Whitey" Kapsalis

Enduring gratitude to Yia Yia and Papou Demas and my father, all of whom encouraged me throughout this effort; to Whitey, of course, my hero. The best part of this is reconnecting with you and your family, cuz. To Terri for her passion, smarts, faith and love; to Irene, Nick and Leah for being themselves; to my mother for being the bridge; to our friends at M & M and Cardinal for taking the chance; and to Aunt Bea Freskos for always making me feel like I could do anything.

Ted Gregory

Paul "Whitey" Kapsalis & Ted Gregory

ABOUT THE AUTHORS

Paul "Whitey" Kapsalis is a Sales Representative in the Apparel Industry in Indianapolis, Indiana, where he has successfully built a loyal and lucrative customer base. Previously, Paul owned and built a soccer specialty retail business into the Number 1 Soccer Specialty Store in the country in 2004 (as awarded by US Soccer). Recognized in the Indianapolis Business Journal's "Forty under 40" list for positive contributions, he also won the Indiana Youth Soccer Presidents Award in 2010. In that same year, he won the Indiana Sports Corporation Volunteer of the Year Award. Paul is a Youth Minister and Eucharistic Minister and also serves as chairman of the Bigelow-Brand Charity Advisory Board of the Pancreatic Cyst & Cancer Early Detection Center. He's a soccer coach who, through words and actions, inspires participants to reach for their goals every day. Paul, Sherri and their three children live near Indianapolis, Indiana.

Ted Gregory is a Pulitzer prize-winning reporter at the *Chicago Tribune*. In addition to his newspaper work, Ted is co-author of *Our Black Year*, a nonfiction account of an African-American family's effort to patronize black-owned businesses exclusively for one year. He lives near Chicago, Illinois, with his wife and children.

CREDITS

Cover:	Sabine Groten
Copyediting:	Elizabeth Evans
Layout and typesetting:	Claudia Sakyi

Photos:
Cover: Photographer-Richard Schultz/1988 Arbutus Yearbook/ Indiana University
Page 9:   Andy Kapsalis
Page 29:   Indiana University Archives (P0043170)
Page 31:   Indiana University Archives (P0043192)
Page 51:   Indiana University Archives (P0043172)
Page 53:   Indiana University Archives (P0043203)
Page 75:   Indiana University Archives (P0043167)
Page 77:   Indiana University Archives (P0043199)
Page 111: Indiana University Archives (P0043196)
Page 139: Indiana University Archives (P0043168)
Page 141: Andy Kapsalis
Page 169: Indiana University Archives (P0043187)
Page 171: Indiana University Archives (P0043180)
Page 205: Indiana University Archives (P0043184)
Page 207: Indiana University Archives (P0043179)
Page 223: Deanne Miller